I WAS NEVER HIM

A NOVEL

HUSSEIN ZOHAIR

BookLeaf Publishing
India | USA | UK

Presentation by *BookLeaf Publishing*

Web: www.bookleafpub.com
E-mail: info@bookleafpub.com

ISBN: 9789369538799

First edition 2025

DEDICATION

To everyone struggling—whether silently or out loud—with mental health, I offer you my mind on an open platter, hoping it gives you something you can finally digest and release.

Within these pages are my most personal thoughts and emotions, laid bare in words. It was my way of facing my demons, and I hope this book helps you confront some of yours as well.

ACKNOWLEDGEMENTS

This is an experimental book.

It didn't start out that way, but as time piled on, so did my ambition. To keep me grounded in my words, I have my wife, Ummulkiram, to thank. Her brutally honest feedback on my concepts and storytelling actually led me to scrap a previous book I had already written 150 pages of.

Yes, completely scrapped, and for good reason. It would've ended up as another mediocre attempt at something done to death many times before. Not to say this book is a masterpiece, but hey, that's for you to decide.

Secondly, I want to thank Ummehani, Rashida Jiji, Murtuza, and Bhoomi for their invaluable feedback and proofreading. Without their support, this book wouldn't be as polished as it is today.

Thirdly, a huge thank you to my brother, Ven Manayan, for creating an outstanding cover that perfectly captures what this book represents, and Abdul Qadir, with whom I created the concept of the cover. When readers inevitably do judge this book by its cover, I'm mostly confident their first thought will be, "Ooh, intriguing." InshaAllah.

Fourthly, I would like to express my gratitude to BookLeaf Publishing for believing in my vision and storytelling, allowing me to bring this book from my hands to yours. Without their support, none of this would have been possible.

I also acknowledge that, considering its experimental nature, this book isn't for everyone; but no piece of art will ever be universally praised, besides Mona Lisa—and I'm sure even that has its own share of critics.

PS – By no means am I saying this book is worthy of the stature of Monalisa, but then again, that is up to you to decide.

Finally, I would like to thank the Government of the United Arab Emirates, who will soon provide me with a Golden Visa for this extraordinary literary contribution.

Manifestation works,
manifestation works,
manifestation works...

ABOUT THIS BOOK

The initial goal of this novel was simple: I, Hussein Zohair (your charming author), just wanted to gather all the poems and prose I've written over the years into one neat package. You know, tie it up with a bow, pat myself on the back, and call it a day. But I quickly realised that would be lazy. And if there's one thing I refuse to be—at least in this moment—is lazy.

So, instead of copy-pasting my greatest hits like a *DJ stuck in the 2000s*, I decided to challenge myself. What if I wove all of these poems and stories into an actual novel, with a plot that connects everything? What if I could offer you an experience that wasn't just a compilation, but something cohesive? The result is the book you're holding now—or, if you're on an e-reader, the digital illusion of a book you're holding now.

Now, before you dive in, I should warn you: there's some new content here, too—fresh poems and short stories that you won't find on my blog, Instagram, or anywhere else. And if you *do* happen to find them elsewhere, someone's stolen my work, and I humbly request they be subjected to the harshest punishment imaginable: listening to Andrew Tate's rap career on loop for five days. That'll teach them.

I've always considered myself a writer, but the truth is, I'm more of a seasonal writer. You know, when the stars align and the "creative juices" decide to flow, I sit down and actually write. Unfortunately, those stars don't align all that often, mostly because I'm lazy. Extremely lazy. So, everything I write comes spontaneously, sparked by experiences or whatever mood I'm in, and typically gets scribbled into random notebooks or typed furiously into my phone, laptop, or whatever's closest: my wife's forehead—don't worry, it has enough space.

But this time, I decided not to be *that* lazy. I didn't want to just throw everything I've written into a book and say *voilà!* I wanted this to feel like a journey, with a thread that ties all these works together—something cohesive, something that challenges me to be the writer I've always aspired to be. Did I succeed? Well, that's what you're here for.

And so, here's the deal: you've got two ways to read this book: you can go from Start to Finish as I've intended, following the storyline that connects all the poems and stories, o*r*, if you're feeling rebellious (and I respect that), I can offer you an index of the poems and prose by page, so you can hop around based on your mood. In fact, thanks to my wife's brilliance, I've even categorised everything into "moods," so you can pick what to read based on how you're feeling—ranging from "Kinda Sad" to "Holy Shit, Get Help." Shakespeare, eat your heart out.

So, here we go. Whether you're in the mood for introspective poetry or a dark tale, there's something here for everyone. And yes, you can expect more than a few shades of sadness because, well, that's where I shine. Let's get started, shall we?

INDEX A

PS - I lied, they're all "*Holy Shit, Get Help.*"

Pro Tip - If you find that the back-to-back poems are slowing your progress through the main storyline, feel free to skip a few. It won't significantly impact the plot. However, I encourage you to always read the final poem before the story continues, as it might hold connections that deepen your understanding of the overarching narrative.

That said, I have one request: if you choose to skip some poems, please don't skip A Father. As a father, this poem holds a special place in my heart—it delves into my darkest insecurities. Sharing it with you feels like exposing a deeply personal part of myself, so I'd truly appreciate it if you took the time to read it. Thank you!

You can always open up this book any other time if you only wanted to dive into the poems and just read those. The page numbers have been mentioned for each of the poems for this purpose specifically.

I hope that at least one—or perhaps even some or all—of these poems, painstakingly written with the fountain pen of my agony, dipped into the ink of my bleeding heart, resonate with you someday. As I pour my soul onto this digital canvas, my greatest wish is for you to find a connection, a shared understanding. If that happens, then I've already won.

INDEX B

Alright, now that all of that is out of the way, let's begin
'Happy' reading!

"It was the start of something I didn't know how to finish, yet the finish line was all I could see."

PROLOGUE

January, 2022

What would you do?

What would you do if you were questioned about your faith, your beliefs, your emotions, and most of all, your identity?

What would you do if you were not accepted for who you are, just because you don't fit into the expectations of what you're supposed to be?

What would you do if you had no one to hear your cries, and when someone did, they'd turn away, instead of coming near and offering comfort?

Would you start hating that world? Or would you just continue living your life, knowing that you'll never be accepted for who you are unless you change yourself?

Or would you change yourself to fit the world's image of you, losing who you really are in the process—would you then be able to look in the mirror and recognize yourself? Would you be able to close your eyes and sleep, dreaming happy dreams? Or would your reality, the one you run away from, come hunting you down like a nightmarish ghoul chasing you in your sleep?

What would you do when the very reason you are breathing is questioned? What would you do if your existence, your chance at living and breathing, was at the mercy of someone else?

Would you get angry at this injustice you're being served, or would you cry, or would you plead, or would you laugh or would you try to run or…

I'm sorry. I'm getting ahead of myself. Let me start over. I'm George. And I have a lot of questions, as you can see.

You see, this world—almost all its inhabitants, including you—live in a delusional state. How do I know? Maybe my thinking that almost all the inhabitants of this world are living in a delusional state, without doing any real research, is also another form of my delusion. A false assumption just to prove my point. A white lie for my black heart.

But when I say "delusion," I don't mean that you're all lost in a fantastical dreamland. What I mean is the simplest of things, like when you say, "It's okay, I'll be fine." Delusion. Or "Ah don't worry about it." Delusion. Or "Someday." Delusion.

Your day-to-day is filled with delusion, and you don't even know it. And I don't blame you. It's the world you grew up in. It's the world you live in.

What's my delusion? There are many, but the biggest one is that I will be heard. I believe I will be heard. You will hear me. You will.

WHY IT WORKS:

1. **Engaging Hook**: The opening question immediately pulls the reader in and makes them reflect on their own experiences.

2. **Smooth Transitions**: The flow of questions builds intensity, while the transition to the character's introduction slows things down just enough to create curiosity.
3. **Tone and Mystery**: George's voice is clear—he's a person grappling with big existential issues, but the tone maintains a conversational, almost philosophical feel, which keeps the reader intrigued.
4. **Tension and Delusion Theme**: By focusing on "delusion," you set up the larger theme of the novel, giving the reader a sense of the internal and external struggles they'll encounter.

“Neglect me in the light of my presence, and you’ll forever drown in the shadow of my absence.”

CHAPTER 1

March, 2006

"Why is it always so cold here? Ugh, I'm freezing. Aren't you?" I asked my friend as I rubbed my shoulders, creasing my white shirt.

The classroom was mildly loud, but not loud enough that you couldn't hear whenever the teacher spoke. And she was going about asking all of us questions in this sudden surprise test. I mean, it's a surprise test, so it has to be sudden, but you get what I mean.

And this wasn't any random surprise test—oh no, no— this was an oral test, so we all had to speak up whenever Mrs. Sato pointed at us. Yay.

"Not really, but I'm also used to this." Takeshi whispered back, his eyes fixed on Mrs. Sato.

"Yeah, makes sense I guess." I shrugged my shoulders.

"George." Mrs. Sato's voice cut through the buzzing classroom, but it sounded far away, like it was being funneled through a tin can. "Can you answer question number 24 that's written on the board?" She smacked her white stick on the blackboard behind her, on question number 25, but then again, she wasn't looking back—close enough. Impressive, really.

My throat tightened, my chest heaved under the weight of heads turning and eyes boring into me from all sides, but my tongue… unfortunately decided it wouldn't move, again. Words sat at the tip of it, stuck like a traffic jam in my head, all signals red. I could feel my throat swelling shut, not from fear but from exasperation. *Here we go again.*

"George, can you answer the question, please?" Mrs. Sato's voice grew sharper, more impatient.

The bully—of course, the bully—had to chime in, as always. As usual. Without fail. Without exception. I'm running out of synonyms. Fuck this guy.

"Or maybe he just broken? Y'know, like the TV remote that don't work. Just need a nice little…" Kenji smacked his hands together, followed by an ill-fitting smirk, his voice oozing with that signature arrogance, flanked by his band of loyal hyenas, all four of them waiting for their cue to laugh. And, right on time, they did. A chorus of snickers erupted, and the warmth in my face climbed. Sigh.

Don't react. Don't show them that they're getting to you.

But it's tough when your tongue weighs a ton. When the words you want to throw back at them are trapped inside, writhing against the cage of your lips, or teeth, or gums, fuck do I know how the hell stammering works. I stared at my desk, trying to will the answer out, trying to *be* the person I pictured in my head. The one who never stammered. The one who had a sharp retort, always ready, always perfect.

"Leave him alone, Kenji." It was Takeshi—and thank God for that—my one real friend in this alien place. He stood up, glaring at Kenji like he was about to throw hands if he had to. "Just because your brain works at the speed of a sloth doesn't mean everyone else has to match it."

The class tensed.

"Quiet everyone." Mrs. Sato tried very half-heartedlyto stop the bullying. Part of me still thinks she enjoyed it.

Kenji's smirk faded for a second, but then it came back even sharper, "Oh, look, his *babysitter* has to speak for him. How sweet." The hyenas didn't miss a beat.

I squeezed my fists under the desk, my knuckles going white. *One day, one day I'll wipe that smirk off his face.* But not today. Not in this stupid reality where my words betrayed me every damn time.

Then the ground rumbled beneath us.

Maybe it was just nerves. You know, like how your legs shake when you're about to do something insane? But no. It wasn't me. It wasn't just my nerves. It was the whole bloody classroom.

The trembling grew violent, pencils rolled off desks, papers scattered like frightened birds, and a low rumble turned into a deafening roar. The building itself groaned in pain, like it was about to collapse under the pressure of whatever was coming.

Earthquake.

A collective gasp arose from the room. Mrs. Sato's face went pale, her usual stern demeanour shattered as she barked, "Everyone under the desks! Now!"

But we barely had time to react.

With a deafening crack, the floor beneath split open, tearing the world in half. Screams filled the air as desks and students slid towards the gaping hole, each smashing against the other along the way. The floor was buckling and tilting as though the earth was trying to swallow us whole. And it was.

Two kids fell. Straight down. The floor just... vanished under them. Their screams cut through the chaos as they flailed, grabbing hold of anything they could, fingers clawing at the jagged edges of what remained of the classroom. I couldn't believe what I was seeing. Somehow I was safe cowering under my desk, but then I heard screams coming from right next to me. It was Kenji's friend—Hiro—and Takeshi. My best friend. My heart seized.

Kenji was already at the edge, holding out his hand to Hiro, his eyes wide with terror.

"George! Help me! Please!" His voice wasn't mocking anymore. It was pleading, desperate. Scared.

I should've moved right then. But I didn't. I just stood there, frozen, staring at Takeshi hanging by his fingertips on the other side of the chasm, the distance between them feeling like an eternity. I would never make it.

"George! Please!" Kenji screamed again, tears rolling down his eyes, his voice cracking as though his puberty relapsed.

But I couldn't help him. Not yet.
I have to save Takeshi first. Takeshi, my best friend.

I dropped to my belly and crawled over the cracked, trembling ground. Slowly, steadily, trying to evenly spread out my weight over the creaking, cracking, and crumbling wooden floor. It was tad slanted, so I also had to make sure I didn't slip. I always thought of myself as a hero, but was I way in over my head?

Finally, I managed to reach a few inches from Takeshi. "Takeshi! Now! Take my hand! Now!" My voice, strong in my head but trembling in reality, finally broke through the chaos.

His hand slipped for a second, panic flashing across his face—white as a ghost—as his grip faltered. But I reached him just in time, grabbing his wrist with both hands, pulling him up with every ounce of strength I had. My body strained, my muscles screamed under the pressure, but I pulled him up, my heart racing in sync with the tremors.

Takeshi collapsed beside me, gasping for air. "You… saved me." He panted, staring at me like I was the hero I've always wanted to be.

But it wasn't over. I turned back. Kenji was still there, still holding Hiro's hand, but he was slipping faster as the ground under them started to shake even more violently. "George!" Kenji screamed again, his voice cracking, raw with fear.

I hesitated. I hesitated for too long. I tried moving towards them when—

The floor beneath them cracked even further, a sickening snap that was heard and felt through every morsel of my being, sending both Kenji and Hiro plummeting into the abyss below. Hiro and Kenji's screams echoed as they disappeared into the darkness.

"No!" I reached out, but it was too late. They were gone. The earth had swallowed them whole.

I stumbled to my feet, staring into the void where they'd fallen. My heart raced; my mind numb. I should've helped him. I could've saved them both. But I hadn't. And now… they were gone.

A sharp snap cut through the air, like a whip cracking right next to my ear.

I blinked. The classroom was still. Whole. There was no gaping chasm, no screaming, no earthquake. Just Mrs. Sato, standing in front of me, her fingers snapping in front of my face, and Kenji with his cabal of hyenas giggling behind.

"George? Are you here?"

I blinked again; my mouth dry. The classroom—the real classroom—was exactly the same as it had been. Kenji, still smug in his seat, his friends still snickering. Takeshi, still sitting next to me, no danger, no earthquake, no heroic rescue.

Just my mind. Just another made-up world from the bottom of my unrelenting subconscious; my sweet escape from a bitter world—my comfortable daydream.

"Dreams offer us a life of unfulfilled destinies,
fleeting as they may be."

CHAPTER 1.1

January, 2022

"Why is it always so cold here? Ugh, I'm freezing. Aren't you?" I asked my friend as I rubbed my shoulders, creasing my white shirt.

"Come on, I know the blanket doesn't really help, does it?" I continued, standing up from the creaky wooden chair of 'Ponderland'. "You know, to be very honest, I'm sure this is the last place you expected to be, and on top of that, you're stuck with me. And trust me, buddy, I'm not going anywhere." I smiled, waiting for him to return the gesture.

I knocked on the pale white walls around us as I walked towards my friend. "Do you mind?" I asked as I pulled out a pack of cigarettes from my trousers. "Gracias!" I said, taking out one white stick of doom and put it in my mouth. "You know, I never really was a smoker, but fuck it—who cares? Isn't that what you told me? 'Who cares!' Best advice."

I tapped my pockets, searching for the lighter, but couldn't find it. "Hey man, have you seen my lighter anywhere?" I said, the cigarette dangling on the edge of my mouth, hanging on for dear life, stuck between my dry lips. "Ah, found it." I walked to the wooden table on the other side of his bed and picked it up. "I might be addicted."

I said as I lit the other end of the cigarette. "Or maybe I'm just lying. Either way, smoking is fun." I said and then inhaled the poisonous nicotine in one, long, beautiful drag.

"Don't worry, man, this won't kill you. There's not much you can do about it anyway, and from the looks of it, you and I are going to be here for a long time..." I said as I stared directly at the black-boxed timer hanging on the wall above my head. The black analog numbers within were accentuated by the clean white background they stood in front of—daunting to some, but just numbers to me. For now.

05:30

"So, get comfortable. I'm gonna be by your side throughout, don't you worry." I said as I walked around the bed and sat back down on my chair with my legs resting on the edge of the bed.

"Lucky for you, I'm a storyteller." I said as I pulled out my phone. "Are you ready? I have a few good ones." I added as I scrolled through the notes. "Not this one... nah, not even t—yes, this one." I said, setting the cigarette aside, still lit, burning. "This doesn't have a name yet, but who cares. Let's dive into the world of poetry, artistry, and most of all, the deepest depths of what makes us human—vulnerability. Ready?"

*****

...untitled...

I'm a miserable mess, tired of this ceaseless test,
But you deserve better.
It's true that my heart stops beating,
When I picture you with another.
I'm good with written words,
But my lips are forever mum.
I've failed to give you the simplest of things.
I've failed repeatedly.
I don't learn, everything burns & everything's the same.
I'm back at it again, crying for attention, chanting your name.

But you deserve so much more.
Oh, I cannot tell you how much I adore,
Your smile, that happiness,
Your love through kindness,
Your care with blindness,
Your love, your everything, you're my highness.

You are my star, my moon.
You're my everything, even in this monsoon of my tears,
trapped within this blackened room,
Through my hatred, my fears and all of the doom and gloom.

I love you so much, but I am a failure.
I try to be better and then I fail here,
At the simplest of things.

My choices aren't binary, like heads or tails, but this coin continues to spin indefinitely.
I strongly believe that I'll always end up on the wrong side of the coin.
So, here I am, writing this pathetic song, asking you to join,
Me on my promenade of mediocrity.
So, I can show you how much I love you through the crashing of my love into your soul like the ocean water bellowing from the floor.
And how much I need you, but the problem is me, this I can see and this needs to be cleaned, but I'm like a ruptured spleen, in pain. Here we go again.

My heart aches.
My smile breaks.
My eyes stutter.
My lips shake.
My hands shiver.
I'm in pain.
Because of you.
Because of me.
Because I'm no good to you.
And you're everything to me.

Time & again I fail you.
Time & again you cry.

Time & again I disappoint you.
Time & again I lie.
That I'll be better next time.
But here we are again.
I'm the same again.
You're in pain again.
Nothing's changed again.
I've still not learned.
Your love, your trust I've still not earned.
Your heart's broken.
I've let you down again.
I said things would be different.
But they've stayed all the same.
We're the same again.
You're in pain again.

*****

"So? What do you think? Not bad, eh? I mean, it's not the strongest of starts, but why should I give you my best from the get-go, right? Let's build it up! That's how you sell a good movie—there always needs to be a crescendo. That's how you'll remember." I rambled on, the cigarette smoke pouring out of my mouth, in thick, chimney-like clouds. My poor lungs.

"Twas but a little love poem I wrote after upsetting my lady. I know, I know—it's more of an apology than a love letter, but the apology comes only because I love her, right? You only feel sorry for the people you truly love, and you only ever admit to a mistake that you never made when you're in love. That's pretty obvious, isn't it? Eh, what would you know." I said as I tapped his hand and pulled out the cigarette from my mouth, holding it in my left hand as my right hand continued to scroll through the umpteen poems I had written on my excuse for a phone. It was more of a diary anyway—a diary of another sullen poet, struggling to deal with his real-world problems. So, he falls back into his safe space, where he can finally read between the lines, dictating it along the way.

"Ready for another one? I'll find you something that's less… lovey-dovey. You never were a fan anyway."

I quickly browsed through my phone to skip to another one of my recent poems. "I think you'll like this one. And it also has a title—hah. How about that?!"

I took one long puff of the cigarette, blowing the smoke up in the air. It swirled around the room, gently smashing against the prickly ceiling before dissipating—the numbers from the black-boxed timer still visible through the thick cloud of my inevitable death.

05:23

"Ready? Not like you have a choice."

*****

...send help...

9:35am
Coffee was hot, but tasteless.
He tries adding a little sugar.
Still tasteless.
He sighs and walks out of the kitchen.
Gazes upon the gloomy weather outside.
It still wasn't as gloomy as his mind.
He takes a sip, tries to wash down the almonds his mother left him on the table.
Takes another sip to wash down the lump in his throat.

6:23am
His mother wakes up.

6:45am
His mother walks into the kitchen.

7:01am
His father wakes up.

10:07am
She's still in bed.

7:30am
His mother's prepared breakfast for everyone, again.

7:00am
His alarm rings.
He shuts it off and tries to sleep.
She slams her palm down on his face.
Demands him to move their son, who made her face his seat.
He unwillingly gets up and tries to get his son off.

She responds with a scoff, because he was late to do as asked.
Alas, another day begins with the fist clasped.

8:10am
His father is playing with his son, while he tries to sleep, but was left undone.
She slams her palm down on his face and demands a report on their son.
He gets wild, angry and yells.
She tells him to stop being rude and just do as she tells him.
He unwillingly gets up and walks out on her to go check on his kin, an irritation starts crawling beneath his skin.

9:00am
He steps out onto the balcony.
It's gloomy still.
He's three storeys up.
A fall could potentially kill.

9:20am
He's making coffee, stirring the spoon to get it right.
He offers to make one for his mom, but she refuses.
She asks him why they were yelling.
He says sorry and continues to stir the spoon of excuses.

10:30am
"She doesn't know the shit I'm going through,
But I don't even know how to put it through to her.
I cannot articulate my emotions as well as she does.
I am always left dumbfounded.
I feel surrounded… by hate."
He says as he sips another sip from his steaming hot cup of coffee.
While staring at her menacingly.
He burns his tongue.

12:00pm
His mother asks about her.
He says she's sleeping still. A long night for her.
His mother asks him about his therapy, if he was able to stop the crying.
He says it's useless; he feels no different, but he was lying.

TWO DAYS LATER

Newspaper Page 4. Side Headline.
Woman Found Dead In Bed; Strangled. Murderer Hospitalized And In Coma. 3 Storeys Didn't Kill.

2:00am
He's alone in the room, handcuffed to the bed.
Peace. At last.

His son, an outcast.

*****

"You know something? That one sent shivers down my spine when I first penned it. Still makes me a little uncomfortable, to think that such thoughts actually run rampant in my head, you know? Like I'm some unhinged serial killer. But… I'm not." I said, rising from the chair. "I'm not!" I tossed the cigarette away angrily, watching it crash against the wall and falling to the ground.

"I-I don't want to feel this way, y-you know? I hate it." I said, as my hands started shaking a little and my heart began to beat faster than usual, reminding me of the first time I felt that way—when I stood shakily above the fallen remains of my bully. Did I say *dead*? I didn't mean dead—I meant he had fallen on the ground, his body in pain and his ego dead. Never did he expect a skinny kid to hit back and hit back *that* hard. Almost dislocated his jaw with that one punch and nearly got suspended from school. Lucky for me, no one believed that I could do such a thing, not even the teachers. I won, but I also lost a piece of me that day; I lost that peace in me. Anyway, I digress.

I continued talking frantically, "I've been feeling such negative emotions most of the time—no, all the time.

Just anger, sadness, emptiness. It keeps eating me alive, you know? Like, my body wants me to just give up. I'm so tired, I feel hollow. I feel no positivity. I just cannot see anything in my life and think it'll turn out good. I just have to…" I walked over to the thrown cigarette and crouched down to pick it up. "… always assume the worst in everyone and everything." I said, staring at the fallen cigarette, now comfortably placed between my fingers.

"Do you know how that would feel? To live like this every day? Everything I write *has* to have a bad ending. I just cannot force myself to write something happy. I'm a writer—I'm supposed to be able to write about anything. But my pen is chained to my feelings and my feelings are limiting me and my perspectives on life. I'm trapped." I said as I took another drag from the cigarette, still sitting in a crouched position. "Trapped like you." I got up and pointed at him. "I hope you're starting to see things more clearly. But I digress. I was here to tell you stories and entertain you. I'm sorry, I got carried away by these stupid feelings of mine, you know? I think I do a better job of telling all this through my poems and stories. Let me tell you another story." I looked up at the black-boxed timer.

05:10

"I think we have the time." I said as I walked and sat back down on the chair next to the bed.

"This one's called *Addicted To Depression.*"

*****

...addicted to depression...

I think... I think I'm addicted.

We are all addicted on some level, to something or someone. Cigarettes, alcohol, social media, drugs, that guy, that girl, porn, these are common.
But there's one kind of addiction that isn't spoken about often.
Or maybe it is, but it's not associated with addiction.
That's depression.
I think I'm addicted to it. Or the feeling of being depressed. Or the thought of being sad. Maybe I just like to feel bad, like a morose grandad who plays throw on his own, because his once-loving children haven't come home to wish him Happy Birthday, fifth time in a row. It hurts... I seem to like it but.

Sigh

What is depression?
Is it a lack of happiness? Or the depth of your sadness?
Or the range of your sadness?
Or the pain of your sadness?
Or the rain of your tears?
Or is it a cumulative effect of your fears?

Or is it the lack of compassion from your peers?
Or is it that you just don't have anyone that can hear you repeat your sad story every time, every year?
Like a little stammering boy, repeating the same words over and over again.
Hoping to maybe move on but still stuck in chains.
For how long can I hold someone's attention.
When I keep conveying the same pain.
And so, like broken and fragile strands of hair, it all gets washed down the drain.
As I stand in the shower, water dripping to my feet from my brain.
My veins pop as the same embarrassing memory flashes before my eyes.
I cry but the water washes away those tears through the rivers forming on my chest all the way down to my thighs.
I'm kneeling in the tub, wondering if I tried, could I drown in that water and die?
Can't you see?
I'm suffering! But do I like it?
Why can't I move on? Why am I stuck on this "why" skit?
Why am I only questioning my grit?
Why do I feel like dry spit?
Useless.

I guess I'm a mess, always distressed, and I need you to caress, I need you to assess, I need you to help me express what I cannot process, and again I regress into feeling undressed, naked, wandering, pandering, meandering and slandering my own attempts at success; unless… I stop digressing and address that I am what I am because I repress, because I suppress, because I'd rather bench press than confess that I really, REALLY, am a horrendous mess.

Sometimes it feels like I'm just rambling on, like a looping song that you loved the first time, maybe second too, but now the same tune annoys you and you want it out of your head, making you restless in your bed.
Time ticking slowly but loud.
There's a black cloud that follows me around, showering and thundering over me like an angry bully and I fully sully my own name and that's my fame, my shame.

But once again I ask the same question:
Why is it that I need depression?
Why is it that I need to feel this tension in my mind, body, and soul?
Why do I want to feel cold? Why do I want to be told you'll be okay, don't worry, we love you? Why do I crave your attention, your worry, your care? Why do I seek your appreciation, your love, your prayer?

Maybe… like a frightened little gay child in an orthodox Muslim family, I feel like I don't belong. Or maybe like a soul is to a body, I string along my depression; as though I need it to survive, so I can feel alive.

But the truth is… I'm just scared to feel elated. I'm scared to feel happy. I'm scared because I know it's temporary.

I'm scared because I know happiness is always in a hurry. Happiness is an expectation of eternal peace, and piece by piece we, try to make it whole. But I fear when it crumbles, it'll leave a deeper hole. It'll hurt less when you fall to your face from the ground, rather than the roof of a skyrise you just found. It's the pain of loss I fear, the feeling of defeat. And I concentrate so much on "what-if", I forget that I decide where I plant my feet, my seed.

I decide what my next steps are. Good or bad, but I'll not hope for a shooting star to save me or help me because I need to help myself; and so, I promise to replace pessimism with optimism on my shelf and stand fearless in the face of defeat, because, like in a videogame, a game over is just a chance to try again… this time with a stronger belief.

*****

"Wait, wait, don't close your eyes. I have one more poem. ***Very***, very similar to the last."

I stood up from my chair, my voice still trembling as I forced a smile. I sat on the bed, right next to his face—so close, in fact, that I could feel the cold, frozen air radiating from it.

"Listen, I gotta keep you entertained. I ***need*** to keep you entertained. You know how much is riding on me keeping you entertained? My entire life. Everything I am. You know that, don't you? Don't you?" My voice cracked, and before I knew it, my hands had gripped his shirt collar, pulling his limp body towards me as I screamed straight into his swollen eyes, "**DON'T YOU?!**"

His lifeless gaze stared back, unresponsive.

"What the fuck is going on?" A voice interrupted from the doorway. It was her—standing there, frozen, aghast. She must have seen the look in my swollen eyes, the madness coming undone.

"What does it look like?" I asked, still clutching his shirt like it was the only thing tethering me to sanity.

Her face paled. "What the fu—" Before she could complete her sentence, I dropped him, his body falling back like a sack of bricks. Slowly, I walked towards her, the weight of my steps increasing with every single step—a stomping darkness followed, "You know how important this is, right?"

"I—I mean…" She seemed a little flustered, her hazel eyes open wide, staring at me with surprise. Maybe she wasn't fully convinced of my methods. Her eyes spoke a different language than what her mind wanted to express. Her lips though, couldn't speak at all.

"You weren't supposed to come in here." My voice was low, a quiet fury simmering within.

"Yes, but… I heard screaming and things breaking." She was lying. Nothing broke, and I hadn't screamed—at least, not loudly enough for her to hear. But I was done explaining myself.

"It's nothing. You know I have to do this, so, please… let me." I said as I stepped closer, gently but firmly guiding her out of the room. "Please, just let me be. It'll be fine." I said for the last time. The door creaked shut, and in that thin sliver of light, I could see tears in her eyes as the light from the room slowly faded into darkness on her face. Such a baby. Good, no more interruptions.

I turned back to him, forcing the door's echo to fade into silence. "Sorry about that. Just a little distraction. Hopefully not again. So, shall we continue?" I said as I walked back towards the bed and sat next to the chair, my voice much calmer now.

"Now, where was I?" I paused dramatically. But I was lying. I knew where I was; I just didn't want him to know. "Ah yes, I have another poem, very similar to the one you just heard. Care to listen to one more? Of course, you do." I said as I sat down on the chair.

"I call this one, *Breakaway*."

*****

...breakaway...

Growing up, I never noticed the trees.
The plants, the grass, the soft whisper of leaves.
It all blended into the background,
Just nature being nature beyond my balcony.
I could see the sea from my window,
But it was nothing significant—just there, distant,
Like the clean air I breathed, the open sky I ignored,
While I watched ants steal candy like it was all that mattered.
Back then, we didn't care for the things we now crave.
Isn't that how it always goes?
We take it all for granted,
Blind to the gifts of life until they slip away.

Then the sea disappeared, swallowed by towers rising like ambitions,
The tree outside my window fell to the grind of progress.
Just another building, another monument to concrete dreams.
The air that once carried freedom now thickens with fumes,
As cylinders and engines hum their mechanical song.
With every new addition to this brand-new world,
We're left with fragments of what was.
Nature, a distant echo we barely hear anymore.

Now, older, I ache for the green, the stillness of the blue seas.
But is it the loss of nature I mourn,
Or the prison of responsibilities I built around myself?
Am I running from this jungle of steel and stone,
Or from the weight of a life I no longer can bear?
Am I seeking refuge because I'm too weak to endure another thrill,
Or am I just afraid of the silence that comes with standing still?

Whatever it is, I'm tired.
Tired of cafés, tired of malls.
Tired of waking up at six to chase it all.
I don't want to be boxed in anymore.
I don't want to groom myself for others' approval,
Or live under the judgment of every word I say.
I don't want to hide behind my fear of meeting every new face,
Afraid of what they'll think, afraid every passing second.
I want to live without this veil of insecurity.
I want to hear your stories, your truths, whatever life beckons.
Not just the triumphs but the losses too.
I want to know every inch of you.

Tell me everything—your joys, your pains.
Let your life's roar fill this emptiness inside me,
So I can break these chains I've bound myself in,
These legal, social, mental shackles that keep me stuck,
Staring at glass walls where once there was green.

If the world can evolve, why can't I?
Why can't I step out of these shadows of my darkened life,
Why am I so afraid of dying without having truly lived?
They say I've achieved so much, but I feel nothing.
What have I done to earn love's gentle touch?
I've stumbled through life,
Fumbling my way to victories I barely believe were mine.

My fear follows me everywhere I go,
Filling me with dread on this lonely road.
Even when I'm supposed to rest, my mind runs wild—
Always building new towers of anxiety,
Constructing worlds of panic and fright.
Of chaos and disarray.
Of darkness in my way.
Of madness that ensues.
Of poetry I reuse.
Of dissatisfaction in my life.
Of this satisfaction cutting with a kni—
Breathe.

I just need to breathe.
To slow down, to see clearly.
Life, like clutter, overwhelms when seen all at once.
But step by step, piece by piece,
I can dismantle the chaos of my days, weeks, and months.
One problem at a time, one burden lifted.
This weight doesn't have to crush me,
I can choose to love, to persevere without hate.
Breathe again. It's not too late.

*****

I was upset. No, scratch that—I was *visibly* upset. He could see it. Hell, I could *feel* it. My skin was buzzing, my heartbeat pulsing through my temples. I didn't like this poem, not anymore. It felt wrong, like a slice of pizza you once enjoyed but now couldn't stomach. Hearing it aloud stripped away whatever thin veneer of worth it had. It was so... childish. So amateurish. So pathetic.

I hated myself the second the last line left my mouth. *Why? Why did I ever think this was good?* My mind spiralled into a whirlpool of disgust, as if every flaw, every awkward word, and shallow metaphor was slapping me in the face, one after the other. My chest tightened, and I could feel that familiar knot of shame twisting in my gut. I could feel his eyes on me too—watching, silently judging, even if he said nothing.

"Uh... I am not a big fan of this poem, to be very honest. I... uh..." My voice cracked, as if I was confessing to a crime. I started twiddling my thumbs—desperately trying to hide their trembling. My body was betraying me, breaking down before my own words. I paced across the room, my steps uneven. My hands clenched and unclenched, clammy and useless, like I was trying to squeeze something invisible that had slipped from my grasp—my sanity.

Salty beads of sweat trickled down my brow, stinging my eyes, collecting like raindrops at the ends of my eyelashes. I could taste the bitter tang of fear on my breath, as if the room itself had become a furnace, amplifying every insecurity.

"I have better ones, I swear." I stammered, more to myself than to him. My fingers kept moving, twitching.

Maybe it was a nervous tic, or maybe I was trying to claw away at the humiliation creeping up my throat—because I really, really hated the poem I had just read out.

My mind raced. I needed to *fix* this. "Wait—maybe we can take a break from the poems, yeah? No more poems." I added, my voice rising as if I had stumbled upon some brilliant solution. It was more of a plea than a suggestion, as if I was begging for mercy from my own self-doubt.

I stopped pacing, spinning on my heel to face him. He was still lying there, unmoved, unreadable. His expression remained a mystery—too still, too quiet. Did he agree? Did he feel what I was feeling? Or was he just watching me unravel, waiting for the next act in my sad little play—or perhaps my next outburst?

"You want to hear a story?" I blurted out, a fake grin plastered across my face. Anything to salvage this moment, anything to distract from my pathetic display. *Yeah, a story,* I thought, *stories are better.*

The words tumbled out of me like I had just found salvation. My whole body felt electrified again, like I had been granted a lifeline. "I have some fun stories to tell too!" I continued, forcing a sense of enthusiasm into my voice. *Fun stories,* I thought bitterly, knowing full well they weren't *fun* in the traditional sense. No, they were the byproduct of my confused, tangled mind—convoluted, erratic, fragmented tales that drifted in and out of coherence like dreams.

Okay, maybe I'm giving myself too much credit. Not all my stories are convoluted. Some are very straight, direct, and to the point, and then there are others—the ones that take you by the hand and drag you down into the rabbit hole, my rabbit hole, kicking and screaming, leaving you unsure of where you'd end up. This next one? Yeah, it falls under the latter category.

"Listen, this one's good." I said, a spark of something—hope? Desperation?—flickering in my chest. I stepped closer, leaning in as if to share some grand secret. "Got a weird name too." I added, with a grin that probably looked more like a grimace. My heart was pounding now, but this time with something else. Anticipation. Fear. *Please let this be good,* I thought, clinging to the last shreds of my confidence, desperately hoping this story would save me from myself.

"Ready?"

*****

...flabbergastation...

***H**ave you ever wondered what would happen if a bee stung its own stinger? Would it implode? Or would it explode? And what about rocks—if you slammed a rock on that bee, would it fly away before you could hit it or would it wait and let you crush it? Does a bee get insomnia? Do they even sleep? What do they do at night? What is their life? ROB— I don't know if I will ever understand a bee's life. It's EXCU— so excruciating to think that I can never fly like th— ROBERT!*

"Huh?" I asked, flabbergasted.

"You may go in now." Said the receptionist, breaking me out of my daydream.

"Oh, okay. Uh… thanks." I said as I scrambled for my papers, bag, mobile, water, tea – I spilled the tea.

"I'm so, so—" I tried to apologize for the fuck up but I couldn't even do that properly. Tongue twisted; body twisted.

"It's alright. The cleaner will get it." The receptionist said, leaning over the desk which seemed too high for her. Probably a new employee, perhaps replacing the previous receptionist for whom that reception was built. Probably someone taller. Could be a woman as well, but that's a very man-friendly height. How sexis—

"Robert! Through that door." She broke me out of my monologue. Again. Maybe she should be replaced soon too.

"Alright, alright. I'm going." Why was Khadija acting like my mom?

I walked towards the glass door and tried to push it open. Guess what? It opened. What did you think? I'd push a 'pull' door? I'm not gonna stumble that mu— I tripped but didn't fall. Caught my fall by holding onto the cold leather chair in front of me. To make matters a little worse, someone was sitting in that chair, and I happened to help spill their glass of water on the table… and on their laptop.

"I am so sorry." I said as I walked around, doing my best not to make eye contact with whoever was sitting on that chair.

"The water is on my laptop!" She exclaimed. A little too loud. Why was she being so dramatic? It's just water.

I walked around someone who was leaving the room – by 'walked around' I mean bumped my soldier into their outer cave curve. Why am I talking like a 5-year-old? I basically grinded against them as they left. And he wasn't even pretty.

I finally got around to my seat, without making eye contact with almost anyone. Ignorance is bliss—SHIT! There she was. My ex. How could this day possibly get any worse? She was sitting right across from me. She was the one whom I ran into when I walked in… stumbled in. She was the one whose laptop got wet because of me. She was the one whose life got better after leaving me for this other rich mother fucker…

WHOWASSITTINGATTHEFARENDOFTHETABLE! WHY THE FUCK AM I HERE?!

This day couldn't get any worse. It really, quite possibly, could not get any wor—

"Robert, thanks for joining us." My ex's smug new boyfriend said through his smug mouth.

"Uh... no problem." I replied, still unsure of quite a lot of things that were going on in that room, in that office, and in my life in general.

"Rebecca has told us so much about your stuff." Stuff? Is he a high schooler? "So, whip it out. Let us see what the big deal is." I was quite certain he was talking about my dick.

"I hope she didn't hype it up too much." I said as I popped open my briefcase.

"Just the right amount, as always." Rebecca said, in her sultry voice. I could almost picture her naked.

"Heh— uh, yeah. So..." I 'whipped' out the small device... that, now that I could see it, did resemble a deformed African penis. Circumcised though.

Apart from the three people communicating in the room, I started getting the feeling that the others were just silent observers. Observers without any eyes, or nose, or mouth, it just looked like their faces had these blurred pencil lines. I felt a little chilly. Probably the AC was turned up. I could feel my nipples getting harder, trying to drill a hole through my thin linen shirt. Thank God for the blazer on top.

Suddenly, everyone else's faces in the room began to blur and fade, replaced by moving 90s desktop monitors playing a static-filled TV channel on mute. The room was eerily silent, visually chaotic, and very, very cold.

"That... is not what I was expecting." The smug new boyfriend said hesitantly as his eyes fell upon my phallic-shaped device.

"It might lo—" Before I could complete myself, Rebecca spoke from the other side, "It's exactly as how I imagined it." Again, saying it in that sexy, sultry voice. That bitch.

I could feel her slipping her panties down under that slim pencil skirt of hers. I don't know how, but I could feel it. As if I were taking off my boxers, but a whole lot sexier.

"What does it do? Give us a brief." The new boyfriend said, smugly.

"This device does move th—" once again, before I could complete my sentence, I was cut off by Rebecca, but this time in person. She had walked up to my chair, her hands playing with my hair, and said, "Just give it to me already." Suddenly I wasn't feeling cold anymore. Quite hot actually; sweaty. Nipples still hard as a hot steel knife.

This was by far the weirdest meeting I had been to. Officially.

"What in God's name are you doing?" The new boyfriend of my ex spoke sense, albeit smugly. But 'sense' was something I was beginning to lose as Rebecca began running her hands down my sweaty shirt.

"Umm... I'm sure this is inappropriate in plenty of states." I said, trying to sound like I wasn't enjoying it. Trying.

"What the fuck is the meaning of this?" The new boyfriend of my ex said, slamming the table with his hands as he got off his smug chair, staring straight at me, smugly.

"Robert! Answer me! What is the meaning of this?" He said with rage in his eyes, blood in his veins, and hate in his tone. But I didn't feel any heat coming off of him, besides the heat in my body at that time, temperatures were soaring because of Rebecca. Her hands had now safely reached my device.

"Robert!"

I didn't care. It felt good.

"Robert!"

Go on, slower, say my name again.

"ROBERT!"

"Huh?" I asked, flabbergasted.

"You may go in now." Said the receptionist, breaking me out of my daydream.

"Oh, okay. Uh… thanks." I said as I scrambled for my papers, bag, mobile, water, tea. I didn't spill my tea.

"Don't forget to take in that phallic-shaped device of yours." The receptionist said, with a smug smile on her smug face.

"How do you know?" I… huh?

"Where do you think you are?" She asked.

"Huh?" I… huh?

"Smile for the camera." A bright white flash went off.

"ROBERT!"

"Huh?" I asked, flabbergasted.

"Smile!" The photographer said. He stood a few feet away from me. Some people surrounded me. I could see Rebecca… and that smug new boyfriend of hers. But I was on a wheelchair. What? Where was I? Why were they taking a picture with me? And where was I? The place looked awfully familiar. White walls. Green floor. Or was it the other way around? I couldn't remember.

"Smile Robert!" The photographer said.

"Smile Daddy!" Rebecca said, looking at me with a smug face. But… was it really smug? I couldn't tell. Also… did she just call me daddy? What? Rebecca…

Rebecca…

Re… Becca… Becka…

Ahh…. Becka… my daughter! Rebecca! I rem—

"ROBERT!"

"Huh?" I asked, flabbergasted.

"You may go in now." Said the receptionist again, breaking me out of my daydream.

"Oh, okay. Uh… thanks." I said as I scrambled for my papers, bag, mobile, water, tea. I spilled it…

"ROBERT!"

"Huh?" I asked, flabbergasted.

*****

"Come on… you have to admit that was good. Wasn't it? Not your everyday story. And as luck would have it, I have another one—very similar and kinda trippy story. Care to listen?" I asked, my voice laden with elation, as I leaned in closer to his face. His eyes, wide and bloodshot, bore into mine. Fear? Anger? Desperation? Maybe all three. I could see the struggle, the silent scream behind his gaze, and it thrilled me. I reached up slowly, my fingers trembling with the thrill of control, and peeled away the tape from his mouth. The sound of it ripping from his skin was oddly satisfying, almost like pulling back a layer of deceit.

"Shhh…" I whispered, dropping the tape onto the floor with a careless flick. "I'm only doing this because I'm getting lonely. I want to talk, but I also want to be heard." My voice dropped to a near-whisper as I took a step back. The air between us felt charged, like a wire stretched too tight, ready to snap. "And the only way for me to be heard… is for you to respond."

I pointed my index and middle fingers, shaped like a hand pistol, towards him, with my thumb raised upwards, reminding me of the black-boxed timer that was still counting down. His eyes flicked towards the timer. We both did.

04:32

"So… what did you think? Did you like it?" My voice was tinged with desperation, not the cool, collected front I had been trying to maintain. I needed him to say something, anything to validate me. His silence, his refusal, would be unbearable.

"It… it's great, George." He whispered, his voice hoarse. A single tear rolled down his cheek, vanishing into the dense jungle of his white and red beard.

"You sure?" I asked again, my stomach knotting. Rejection hung in the air like the sharp smell of ammonia, waiting to strike.

"Y-yeah. It was… so captivating." He said, his eyes red and his lips dry—exhausted. His words sounded weak, fragile, like they could shatter at any moment.

"Good… can I tell you another, please?"

His gaze shifted down to his bound wrists, the ropes biting into his skin, leaving angry red marks. "Ye… yes, but can you also… maybe… loosen these a little?" He stammered, pointing at his hands with sullen eyes.

"I want to… but… no… please stay a while, please." I said, with tears almost filling up my eyes. My tough demeanor was cracking with every passing second. She would notice, and I didn't want her to notice. This had to continue. The show had to go on.

"O-okay… I'll listen." He mumbled, sounding a little defeated, I think. I think we both felt defeated in our own way. Funny. I was supposed to be in control. I was free yet caged. Or was I?

"Thank you." The words left my mouth, hollow, empty. My legs buckled, and I slid to the floor, my back pressing against the cold, grimy wall. The mirror on the opposite side of the room, cracked and fractured, reflected a version of me I didn't recognize. My face, distorted by the broken glass, looked like something from a nightmare. My eyes were bloodshot, and my hands—my hands were a mess. Bruised, cut, streaked with dried blood. *These aren't a writer's hands,* I thought. *These are… something else. Something wrong.*

The room seemed to close in around me, the walls peeling back layers of decaying paint, the air thick with the stench of dampness. Water dripped steadily from a pipe overhead, adding to the suffocating atmosphere. The light flickered, casting eerie shadows that seemed to crawl along the flo—

"Aren't you going t-to tell me another story?" He asked, his voice breaking through the haze, pulling me back to reality. He was still lying there, watching me with those sad, defeated eyes.

"Yes… yes I am." I forced myself to sit up straighter, trying to regain control. I had to tell him. I had to tell him another story. This one would be better. It had to be. "I like this one. It's called *What.*"

He blinked, confusion flickering across his face. "Are y-you asking me?" His voice was small, hesitant, like a child lost in the dark.

"No," I said, a faint smile tugging at the corners of my mouth. "I'm telling you. It's called *What?*" I couldn't help but laugh a little, the absurdity of the situation getting the better of me. The laugh felt wrong, hollow, but it was there.

"Oh, okay." He laid his head back down on the pillow, his eyes fluttering shut for a moment. Was he finally at peace? Or was he just giving up? I couldn't tell anymore.

But something about his small, simple reaction made me nervous. My stomach twisted, and doubt crept in, gnawing at the edges of my mind. *Was I doing something wrong? Was he judging me? Was I failing?*

I hated being judged. I hated it more than anything. But I also craved acceptance. How could you be accepted without being judged? How does that even work?

The questions swirled around in my head, but I pushed them aside. I had to focus. I had to keep going. I had to tell him this next story. He needed to hear it. And maybe I needed to tell it.

I took a deep breath, heart pounding in my chest. "Alright," I said quietly, more to myself than to him. "Let's get started."

*****

...what...

"You're next, Abdul." Carter Jr. said and stepped off the podium, leaving a vacant spot for yours truly.

Oh sorry, I am very bad with introductions. I am Abdul. Abdul Ahsan. I'm an Indian Pakistani – a not-so-rare combination, and definitely not a revered one. I'm sitting in an Alcoholics Anonymous meeting, somewhere in Oman; I can't quite figure out the name – not that it really matters. What's outside this room concerns me at a whole zero, same as much as it concerns you. What matters is right now, right here, in this very room, amo—

"Yo, you're next, go." Shantanu nudged me, suspending me from my internal monologue.

"Thanks." I said, fake smiling my ass off as I got off my chair and slowly walked towards the podium.

"You got this." Sarah, the lovely overweight Arab aunty who always liked me, patted me on my rear-end as I walked past her chair. If she was younger, I'd pat her somewhere too, but nah, not right now.

I walked up to the podium and stopped for a second. My head started pounding. I could feel my ears getting hotter, and my eyes were starting to see what I can only describe as concussion rings floating through the air, smashing into my skull with every beating of my heart. My heart was fine, it didn't hurt, but my head, ohh… my head.

"It's alright, Abdul. I'm right h—" Carter Jr. tried consoling me, but I was in no time for his bullshit.

"I know. I'm going. You don't n-need to be s-s… so pushy." I responded, quite violently. I know I shouldn't have, but I couldn't help myself. I hate these people and their fake concern. He's only doing this 'cause he's getting paid to do this.

"That's not true, Abdul." Carter responded, but this time from behind me.

"What?" I said, looking back. Carter was not just behind me—he was also below me. I was standing on the podium. Did I just blurt that whole thing out… out loud?

"Yeah, you did." Carter Jr. responded, but without moving his lips even a little.

"What the fuck! How are you reading my mind and how are your lips not moving when you're talking?"

"What are you talking about?" Carter Jr. said, looking rightfully dazed. He looked exactly like what I imagined I was looking like in that moment.

"Yo, you're next!" Shantanu nudged me, waking me up from that weird but surreal dream.

"What…" I spoke, still a little dazed from that larger-than-life dream sequence that you and I just went through.

"It's your turn. Carter just got off the podium." Shantanu whispered.

I looked over at the podium and, you guessed it, I saw myself standing right there, about to give a speech.

"What the fuck?" I said, looking at myself standing on top of the podium, five meters away from my steel chair. I stood up on my spot, rubbing my eyes.

"What?" The version of me standing on the podium said, looking back at someone who, to me, looked like… Carter. That's Carter. Wait. Didn't I just see this? This has to be another trippy dream sequence. Cannot be real whatsoever. I'm not that stupid and neither are you. You know what time it is? It's time to pinch myself.

"OW!" That actually hurt. Why'd you imagine me pinching myself in the arm? I have fleshy arms and pinching there just gives me more bruises and blood clots. If you didn't think of pinching me in the arm, then something is probably wrong with me and I cannot align with your thoughts.

Tell me, what are you thinking right now? I'm thinking of rainbows and unicorns running on those rainbows with a… a cat, rolling down the rainbow like a ragdoll. Don't worry, cats have nine lives, so it's all fine.

"OW!" I had to pinch myself again. This dream sequence isn't ending and I'm rambling about things that make no sense. But I guess it's not working, I'm still standing here, looking at myself standing in the crowd of steel chairs. Wait. I was in the crowd of the steel chairs, which means… what the fuck! I'm on the podium!

"Abdul! Do you need help?" I heard a very muffled Carter Jr. call out from behind.

"Huh?" I turned back to him.

"D o y o u n e e d a n y h e l p?" Carter's words came to me very, very slowly.

"Uh… what's going on?" I questioned, with my arms to my sides, standing like a pregnant Superman.

"You just stood still for a good forty seconds on the podium just now." Aha! Carter Jr. to the rescue. So, I ***was*** *dreaming, but from the podium!*

"I'll ask again, do you need any help, Abdul?" Carter Jr. said—he shouted, really. But it wasn't the loud, scolding shout of a parent. It was more like someone trying to warn you of a shark swimming right behind you, under the water. Are you getting me? It's like they're trying to be loud, but the environment around them isn't allowing them to, so they try to be louder with their body language, but I can't read body language to save my life. I once tried asking a girl out for a five minutes straight only to realize she wasn't even listening to me; if only I understood her body language, but I couldn't. You know why?

"OW!" Why'd you do that?

"Because slapping you across your face didn't work!" Carter Jr. said, as he slowly let go of my balls.

"This is harassment!" I replied as he stepped off the podium.

"When Sarah does it, it's flirting, when I do it to fucking wake you up, it's harassment." Abdul replied, a little miffed.

Wait. Why is Abdul talking to me… aren't I Abdul? Man. I'm just going around in circles. I really wanted to tell you guys a good story, but my mind is just not letting me focus. I'm tired of all these distractions, all these… problems… all these… bad news… everywhere. I'm trying to think of something nice, but my mind just doesn't let me. All I have are these bad, ugly, disturbing images in my head of scenarios that should actually be peaceful.

"The world isn't the same, Abdul. Don't worry. You'll be fine." Carter Jr. said from behind me.

"I'm going to turn around and you're going to be me, aren't you Carter?" I said, as I closed my eyes and turned away from the crowd, standing atop the podium.

"Still me, Abdul. Relax, you got this." Carter Jr. said, standing right behind me like a strong pillar – a pillar of support.

That pillar of support was all I needed to stop doubting myself, my reality, my everything. It took a lot of years, but here I am, standing next to this man—this man who has always meant the world to me. Through all my adult years, Carter Jr. was there right beside me, and just like me, he was right beside all of you. He has given all of us more than a reason to live, to stop being ashamed, to stop being worried about what we were. He helped us embrace our "faults". He made us realize that we're normal, like everyone else. The one thing he said that has never left me was this one line that I went ahead and got tattooed on my arm. It reads, "You are who YOU are."

It's such a simple line, but it means so much. We are all who WE are. We aren't a collective of a hive mind or a hive body. We're all individuals. With our own personalities. With our own shortcomings and our own strengths. There is no such thing… thing as "perfect" because "perfect" is a collective decision that a society has accepted, maybe because one person who was the first to think of it, passed it down through generations of funneling.

I'm sorry if I sound like I'm rambling, but all I'm trying to say is, there is no such thing as perfect, because we're all perfect. And when everyone is, no one is, and that is the beautiful world that Carter Jr. has left us all in. I am honored to have known someone like Carter Jr. in my life; a person who walked me through Schizophrenia Anonymous like it was a pre-school nursery. I was a child then. I still am now, but a child that breathes easy.

And with that I'd like to conclude my eulogy. Thank you all for listening to me.

*****

"That... wow." He said, his voice wavering, and eyes glistening with unshed tears. Maybe the story had touched something deep within him, something raw.

"Really?" I leapt up from my cross-legged slump, a surge of joy flooding through me. *Finally,* I thought. *He gets it.*

"Yes... that was something else." He said, his voice cracking. "Can... can you please wipe away these tears? They're making it hard t-to see. Plus, I'm really just feeling itchy." He blinked rapidly, his face contorting as he squirmed uncomfortably.

I wiped my own eyes first, my fingers rough against the tear-streaked skin. "Better?" I asked, gently swiping his cheeks with my bruised, raw hands, the calluses catching against his softer skin.

"Almost. Could you... maybe loosen my hands as well?" He asked again, this time to my annoyance.

I stiffened, irritation prickling under my skin. "Why? So, you can try to kick me out again?" The bitterness in my voice was sharp, even to my own ears.

"No! No-no. I-I want to hear all your stories; I promise I will. But my hands are starting to hurt." He requested, genuinely.

For a moment, I almost felt sorry for him. I shook my head, trying to fight the sudden surge of empathy. "You're ruining my flow, you know that? You were better with the tape on your mouth." I reached down to pick it up, a flicker of amusement curling my lips.

"No, no! Please! No tape, I'll not ask you for anything anymore, I promise. Please, no tape." He said, squirming.

I paused, staring at him for a moment before dropping the tape back to the floor. "Okay," I muttered. "For now."

He let out a shaky breath, relief washing over his features. "It feels good to talk, doesn't it?" I asked, my tone darkening. "Especially when you've been ***denied*** that simple pleasure. Feels different, huh? Makes you appreciate it more." I smirked, pacing back towards the wall. "I love talking to myself. It's a skill, really. You should try it sometime, now that you know how precious words can be."

His lips tried to move, failingly. No sound came out. He tried again, his voice muffled, strained. My smirk widened. *Ah,* there it was—the familiar choke of desperation. There was no tape on the floor.

"I think we're good with stories for now. Another poem, perhaps? Of course. Anything for my best audience!" His eyes widened as I ignored the tension in his wrists, the silent pleading in his gaze. I dug into my pocket and pulled out the cigarette pack. I slid one from its tight paper sleeve, letting it dangle lazily between my fingers as I brought it to my lips—but didn't bite or light it.

"Poems are better anyway," I mused aloud, my voice adopting an almost dreamlike quality. "They're easier to write. No need to make perfect sense. You leave just enough room for the listener to fill in the blanks. It's a cheat code, really. And you know what's beautiful about poetry? It's the purest form of human emotion. Raw. Broken. Fragmented words. Sometimes they rhyme, sometimes they don't. It's a reflection of the mind—disjointed, chaotic. Kind of like this whole situation, don't you think?" I continued to ramble on. My audience didn't heckle, couldn't, and that was something I could count on.

"Anyway, this next poem… oh, you'll love this one. It's called *Belong.*" I glanced over at him, my grin widening. "It's a long one, so don't hold your breath."

I didn't wait for a response as I took a seat, my eyes narrowing at the cracked mirror across the room. My reflection—distorted, warped—stared back at me, the fractured pieces of a man barely holding it together. My fingers twitching against the cigarette, the need for validation, for recognition, gnawing at me. I cleared my throat, leaning forward ever so slightly, and began.

"This one's for you." I whispered under my breath and looked up, staring straight at the speaker above the doorway, staring back at me, motionless, silent yet loud.

*****

...belong...

Do I belong here?
He asked as he gazed upon the chains.
Do I belong here?
His question echoed around the empty room's empty remains.

A rusting chair, a wet bed, and a papered-up window were his only friends. But were they even real?
The white walls don't lie, but how can I trust how I feel?
The tight halls where light falls is quite small, as the night stalls she might call to take me home.
And so, he had to make friends out of nothing.
What else would one do when your brain's filled with stuffing?

He reminisced about the cockatoo he had as a child.
About the happiness it brought him, an unending smile.
He couldn't live a day without it, and so, kept it close.
Shut away in its cage, meanwhile, he strutted along his day as planned.
Came home and had just one demand.
"I want to see Poly, my best friend."
And Poly would chirp and cheer when he'd come around again.

Though he wondered now, were those sounds of cheer?
Or were they filled with fear? Or worse, anguish?
"Did Poly love me? Or was it afraid?" Never could distinguish.
The answer was neither. This cockatoo was a fighter too, but poly was meant to fly free.
Build a home in a tree. Fly across the empty sea.
Be who she was truly meant to be.

But because of the love the boy had for her, Poly had to forget those dreams.
Had to forget the river streams.
She had to forget the sound of rustling leaves blowing away from the wind born out of her wings.

This cockatoo would gawk at who? A Hawk she knew as it flew above, trying to mock her too.
So, it'd walk a few circles around its constant view.
But the time had come to slump,
'Cause Poly had to forget freedom.
How to forget though? Forgetting isn't easy.
On occasions, she would fly away and get lost.
Come back home later that night as the boy would be aghast.
Calm him down with a few chirps, bringing him glee.
"You never were lost, were you? You tried to flee."

The boy knew now what he didn't before.
He caged the one that he adored.

He caged her because he was afraid to let her go.
And she came back every time because she loved him too.
He would sacrifice his time, his friends, and his life.
And come home running too.
But never once did he wonder if Poly wanted it all.
Did Poly want to stay home?
Did she want to be caged?
Did she want to be my friend?
Or did she want it all to end?
These questions never entered his mind.
He was blinded by his love to truly see.
That slowly and steadily, he was killing Poly.
She was strong, looked after, and well-fed.
But emotionally, she was already dead.

One day, he came home, high on delight,
Until his eyes fell on Poly, her neck twisted tight.
He cried, he cried until his tears ran dry,
Cried until the echo of his voice could no longer fly.
He cried until he had no more breath,
And Poly lay silent, cradled in death.
His family came, held him through the night,
But nothing could bring back that joy, that light.
Her cries still echoed in his restless dreams,
Haunting him, tearing at his seams.
Weeks passed, and a new bird took her place,
But Poly's memory? Now erased without a trace.

Do I belong here?
His mind thought, but his lips were sewn shut.

Do I belong here?
The question lingered till his lips were cut.
He spoke out, tearing the restraints.
It hurt, but he'd do it again.
He couldn't fathom the pain he'd put someone else through.
He now knew the pain he had caused,
The agony of being trapped, the misery it embossed.
Was this his punishment?
Karma doing its thing.

Never did he know he'd resent something he craved,
Never thought he'd want to tear down the walls he'd paved.
Never knew he'd reach a point of no return.
His mind on a cliff, his hand on a gun.
There's no way out without being branded wicked.
Might as well blow his own head.
At least then, he won't have to deal with the ramifications of his actions.
At least then, he'd have a quick exit without being shunned.
At least then, they'd know why he had done what he had done.
At least then, they wouldn't spit on his name.
At least then, they wouldn't get to claim,
That he was a no-good man.
He was good, but couldn't fit the plan,
That someone else had set for him.
His cuffs rattled and bled through every limb.

Do I belong here?
He asked, silently to the wind.

I don't belong here.
The line between reality and fiction thinned.

*****

"I know, another sad story. I know. But unfortunately, that's all I can think of. Like, I try to make my sadness kind of interesting, but I also know this makes me look like a one-note writer. And kind of a bad one at that too, 'cause if I weren't bad, we probably wouldn't be here, now, would we?" I said with the cigarette between my bruised fingers, still unlit.

"And you know the worst part?" I leaned ahead, finally putting the cigarrette between my dry lips and lighting it.

"I've tried to write happy shit so… many… times." I said inhaling a long puff. Ah, bliss. My lips were cracked from the dryness and the nicotine definitely wasn't the moisturizer I needed. "But it never felt natural. Always forced." My words came out full of smoke.

"I want to be honest to myself. I want to be honest to my emotions. To my craft. I cannot write something I don't believe in." I said, the cigarette hanging between my fingers as I blew smoke into the room, thickening the air with each puff. My chest felt tight, not from the nicotine, but from the pressure building around me.

That's when I heard it—a sharp knock on the door.

"Who's there?" My voice came out more frantic than I intended.

"Frida! Who else?" Her voice echoed through the crack in the door, strained, on edge.

"NOT. NOW!" I snapped, biting down on the words.

"YOU NEED TO STOP THIS! IT'S GOING NOWHERE!" Her voice too grew louder, more desperate, breaking through the thick walls like needles piercing my skin.

"I TOLD YOU TO LEAVE ME ALONE!" I roared, throwing the cigarette to the ground, stomping it out as I stormed towards the door, my pulse rising with each step.

I could feel him squirming on the bed behind me. He knew something was wrong.

"Don't you get any ideas, you hear me?" I yelled, pointing at him with my trembling finger trying its hardest to hover in the air like a threat. "Stay there, don't move, be lifeless, motionless. You're perfect that way. *Perfect.*"

I turned back and flung open the door to reveal Frida standing there—her eyes burning, her lips pressed tight, and in her hand, a gleaming pair of scissors. *Sharp ones.*

"What the fuck do you think you're doing?" I asked.

Without missing a beat, Frida barged into the room, her eyes locked onto the man tied to the bed. "This has gone on long enough!" She shouted. "I cannot continue to be a part of this." Frida walked up to the bed.

"No, no, no, no!" I lunged at her, worried.

She spun on her heel, the point of the scissors glinting under the bright white light. "Back off!" Her voice wavered, but her grip on the scissors was firm. She pointed them at me like a weapon, her hand trembling but resolute.

"Frida, please… I just need a little more time." I said, my hands raised, trying to calm her down and make her understand MY FUCKING SITUATION!

"More time?" Her eyes bore into mine, filled with a mix of frustration and sorrow. "Where do you think this is going? Where?!" Her hand shook as the scissors wavered between pointing at me and George on the bed. Sweat glistened on her brow, her breath quickening.

"Just… some more time." I tried to reason WITH THIS FUCKING BITCH! ARGH I WAS SO MAD!

"No more, please Jason. No more!"

"WHO THE FUCK IS JASON?" I asked. "My name is Jeffery!"

"What?" She looked perturbed.

"Are you okay?" I asked as I took a tentative step closer, lowering my voice as if to calm a frightened animal.

"Ye-yes… Stand back!" She noticed me take another step.

"What is going on, Frida?" I asked her, as my steps continued their pursuit.

"STOP GETTING CLOSER!" She screamed; the scissors now pointed directly at George's throat. The blade hovered dangerously close, her hands trembling.

"Okay, okay." I quickly took several steps back. "Please don't hurt George." I said.

"Hurt him? Why will I hurt him?" She asked, confused. "And *your* name is George!" Her voice cracked again, splintered with confusion.

"I am not George. He is George." I gestured to the man on the bed. "I am Jeffery. I am not Jason either." I said, with my arms still up.

"Who is Jason? What's happening?" She asked, her face pale.

Something went wrong. If this issue [illegible] ....

"I… don't fucking know." I responded as calmly as I could.

She stared at me, lost in a whirlwind of emotions. Then her gaze hardened again, "Forget it. I'm cutting him loose, enough is enough!" She quickly started cutting the tape around his hands.

"NO!" I roared, bolting towards her. My body slammed into hers, throwing her against the wall with a sickening thud. The scissors clattered to the floor.

She fought back, her fists pounding against my chest, her knee driving into my gut. But I was stronger. I pinned her, dragging her towards the door. Her head snapped back, crashing into my face, breaking the grip I had on her.

As I stumbled a few feet, she quickly ran and picked the scissors up from the ground. Instead of running towards George, she charged at me.

"FRIDA!" I yelled, my voice tearing through the air like a warning shot, raging.

She ran at me, scissors raised. There was no time to think. Just *react.*

We collided—her body slamming into mine, the force sending us both crashing to the floor.

The sound of tearing flesh echoed in the room. Her weight collapsed on top of me. I gasped, feeling the cold steel pierce my side. My hands fumbled to push her off, but she was heavier now, dead weight.

"George..." Her voice was barely a whisper, her lips coated in blood, her breath ragged and shallow.

"Frida..." I breathed, my hands trembling as they pulled away from her limp body—slick with blood.

The room spun. The mirror on the wall fractured under the weight of my gaze. I could see my reflection, distorted and broken, my hands soaked in red—her blood, my blood. It didn't matter anymore.

Everything was still, except for George's eyes, darting between me and her like a pendulum of terror, each swing amplifying the frantic beat of his petrified heart.

*****

"The war between right and wrong doesn't settle the dust; it stirs the soil for new sins to bloom."

CHAPTER 2

January, 2022

Her silence was deafening now, louder than any scream could ever be.

"Frida?" I murmured, a soft, almost gentle slap against her face, but her head lolled against my shoulder like a broken doll. Her skin, once warm, was now cold against mine.

"FRIDA?" I shouted, shaking her, but she hung there, limp, lifeless, her body sagging like a hollow shell. I glanced up at George, that little rat squirming in the bed. Oh, he was still moving. Still breathing. Still alive. Unlike Frida. Very much dead.

Her last breath clung to my neck, chilling my spine like the arctic wind slicing through the thickest night. They weren't just goosebumps, these were goosehills—hell, goosemountains. So strong. My hands felt like they were holding the final warmth of this world that I knew, slowly disintegrating away, along with my humanity. No. Not my humanity.

I stared at Frida's lifeless body, her chest unmoving, her skin so cold. My hands—stained, soaked, drowning in blood, her blood. Red, deep, dark red.

"STOP SQUIRMING!" I shouted at George, standing so quickly that the room tilted around me. I pointed a trembling, bloodstained finger towards Frida, "LOOK WHAT YOU MADE ME DO!"

But I felt a sudden shift in my emotions, as though I was speeding through the five stages of grief at breakneck pace—my body eager to move on to the next wave of emotions that I wanted to liberate. It was as if I was being rushed—feelings hushed, and the guilt brushed aside. I couldn't get off the ride of disassociation, but at least George was still by my side.

"She never really loved me, you know?" I muttered, sitting back down, my body sinking into the cold beside her. "But I did. Once. Once I did."

I stared at her face. God, she was beautiful, even then. Her hazel eyes—wide, frozen in terror—still so goddamn beautiful. I reached out, ran my fingers down her cheek, caressing her like she was still alive, like she could feel it.

"You must think I'm insane." I chuckled, a low, crazed sound bubbling up from my throat. "But you did this to me."

The laughter came harder now, spilling out of me like a flood breaking through a dam, finally cracked. "You did this to me, you rat! I'm insane because of YOU!" My laughter echoed off the walls, filling the room, bouncing back at me like a mockery.

"And now..." I paused; my voice caught in the wave of laughter that suddenly died in my throat. "Now she's gone."

I turned towards her; my laughter turned to silence. I moved in close and whispered in her ear, "I loved you once, Frida. I did. And I still do. I always will." I shut her eyes with my fingers.

"Well, that's that, I guess. She's finally gone." I sighed as I sat back up, wiping my hands on my not-so-white-anymore shirt. I adorned a canvas of her blood on me.

I turned to George, standing weirdly above Frida's body like a man trying to step over a puddle of water, like her death was just some inconvenience on the way to the next thing.

"So, uh… this is a bit awkward, isn't it?" I grinned, feeling the mania twist and curl inside me. "But ready for another story?" I stepped closer to George, my grin widening as I pointed down at Frida. "I mean, unless you want to end up like her."

I laughed, a wild, hysterical laugh that filled the room, cutting through the tension like a blade. "Relax, relax. I'm only joking. This was... an accident." I leaned in close, my face inches from George's. "Yours won't be. Yours will be murder." My smile disappeared, my eyes dark, hollow.

"Again, just kidding." I laughed hysterically. "But I guess it's time—" I looked up at the timer. My doomsday reminder.

04:09

"—for another poem. And since you've had to wait for so long, let's give you three back-to-back, what do you say? Ready, decider of my future?" I smirked, licking my dry lips.

*****

...death doesn't seem so bad...

Sometimes death doesn't seem so bad.

When you're all you ever had.
When the emotional barometer in your head's been dead stuck on sad.
When your heart only beats to flood your body with blood.
When you breathe only to keep this hopeless crusade of life alive.
When you're already dead inside,
Sometimes death doesn't seem so bad.

Hopelessness isn't a passing feeling anymore.
It's not even a feeling anymore.
It's a leech sucking me sore, permanently stuck before I could realize its nature and now it stays here, dangling onto the threads of my heart.
Sucking away any bits of peace that tried to keep me from falling apart.
Into pieces I fall, yet forced to pick myself up.
Sometimes I just want to lie in the rut,
In the hurt,
In the needling pain of distrust.

In the gurgling of blood,
Cut in my throat through this knife that I call life.
I'm alive, I'm breathing, but my soul is weeping.
I was teeming with hope once upon a time.
Now I just rhyme my sorrows on a pad.
Sometimes death doesn't seem so bad.

Face down, on the ground, pounded into submission.
My face, wrinkled, submerged into a pool of tears.
My eyes dry, like an empty oasis at peak noon.
My lips torn, bruised and bleeding into this spoon,
That I put back into my mouth.
I am my own criminal.
I am my own killer.
I could choose to heal, be a healer,
But I am my own drug dealer.
My drug, depression, my addiction.
Happiness isn't that difficult; I am told as I weep.
It's too late for me now, I am in too deep.
Happiness is difficult because my sorrow is now ironclad.
It's true, sometimes death doesn't seem so bad.

Sun shining down, painting my shadows darker.
I'm farther away from the truth, but I know I'm smarter.
The windows to my heart are closed shut, I don't let anything seep in.
I don't even stand a chance to win, because, to me, it's all the same.
I know this game; I always end up withering in pain.
And God's there, but all he does is watch.

Is he really out there? No, he's not, says the atheist beside me.
We are all gonna die one day, don't you see?
Why do you hold onto this knife so dearly?
Why do you wait for every chance to unload these bullets of hate into your heart?
Why do you keep trying to find ways to fall apart? Do you like it?
Why do you diligently avoid every good grace that comes your way?
No, there is no God, but I still want you to pray.
Pray to yourself, pray to your heart.
Pray to be better for the people that matter.
Pray to be stronger.
We will all die tomorrow, so why waste today?
Because I lack patience anymore, my mind is withering away.
I gaze onto the ground from a mile above,
Sometimes… death is the only way to let go.

*****

...a woman...

I hate this.
This world.
This beautiful green, brown, blue, black, and red world.
I hate it. Sometimes.
Suffocation has replaced respiration.
As my bright sunny days begin,
And as my breathtaking cloudy nights end.
I live with it.
A constant, everlasting chokehold.
Gently, yet firmly placed right around my pulsating throat.
No wiggle room, no space to adjust.
No time to let myself go.

Stress, anxiety, depression—they're no longer strangers,
But daily visitors in my hollow, purposeless life.
And yet, I still chase rainbows every day, every night; still trying to get to that elusive pot of gold.

But as I've been told a thousand times before, that my struggles are truly futile, and in the midst of all this inherent chaos of my mind, I see a message pop up on the mobile.

It's her. My one and only beam of light in these daunting, troubled times.

She's the only sight that truly gives my aging heart, my racing heart, my raving heart some joy, and thus a smile ever so gently creeps up on my aching face at a slow pace when I begin to read the words that she says, staring wide-eyed into the bright, blue-filtered interface of my iPhone. "I'm all alone and I miss you."

I get up from the bed, slowly.
Don't want to wake anyone up.
Still staring wide-eyed into my phone, I make my way into the kitchen, sipping down water, one long gulp at a time, trying to wash down my inhibitions.

"I miss you too" I write back. Dopamine rushing to my head from the thumping of my chest as I make my way back to where I was, on my side of the bed.

"I'm ready" She sent another message. My heartbeat raged, promiscuous, the thumps were so loud I felt it wanting to tear through its cage.
"Tomorrow" I write back and fall asleep. It's finally happening, oh man, I could barely breathe.

The next day, we go to her place straight from work. She's feeling it, I'm feeling it, we're both ready to make it work. She parks her car in the basement, the lights are dim, but I could still see the glimmer in her bright blue eyes as I walk up to her door and let myself in with a shifty grin.

I could hear a waterfall; I could hear birds. I could feel the sun rising on the other side of this Earth. I could feel big blue waves crashing fiercely into a steep cliffside. I could smell the fresh air from the bosom of a rainy forest inside.

I look at her, she looks back at me. Not the first brunette my eyes had ever seen, but the first brunette to make me feel unclean today; so dirty, so naughty, so angsty, I was swayed.

I persuade my lips to put on a smile, in reality, I just want to bite, but there is time for that, and so I hold it in. She smiles back at me, so sultry, and I was ready to sin.
I caress her body gently as our lips lock for the first time. This young, ravishing, blue-eyed brunette with freckles that would make your heart sing, had made herself mine.

The passion is enigmatic, my mind – erotic, and my heart is in pain, because I feel a sense of déjà vu, I feel like I am going to end up hurting someone again.
But in that moment, I let myself go as she swallows me whole. I forget everything else and just know that my role right then was to be hers and only hers, and this she knows too.

Our scents intertwine; our senses are lost. Our breath becomes one, and the threat of rejection is now in the past. She pushes me away, and says that it isn't all that she wants.

I am taken aback for a moment until she opens her bedroom door, letting her clothes fall to the floor, and my jaw follows.

She is better than the powers of my imagination. She gestures me to follow her, and without hesitation in haste, I run inside and put my lips on her beautiful face.

She is already undressed, her body rubbing against a barrier of my clothes and so, she starts undoing mine, and once she is done, she pours me red wine. Ah delicious, her, not the wine.

Her room's dimly lit too; perfect for us. Perfect for the mood— perfect for me to caress her ever so gently as I let the wine pour onto her perfect body… slowly starting to drip on the floor from every inch of her that I adore.

Like a wet umbrella from a rainy day, lying down in a wet alleyway – slippery, dirty, I pick her up. We kiss and walk to her bed with her legs wrapped around me, and my mind around hers.

She murmurs something into my ears and my heart is instantly chained. We fall slowly into love as her silky sheets get stained.

But in the moment of passion, I forget one thing, the vibrations on my phone as it continues to ring.

"Just answer or turn it off!" She says, giving me a little peck. "Forget about it!" I say as I slip inside her and kiss her neck. But something awful happens in the very next minute as she sees who was calling, putting her out of her wits.

"Who is this?" She asks, looking at the name on my phone's display.
"No one important." I tried to take my phone away.
"18 missed calls isn't nobody!" She continues to interrogate.
"Just… fuck it." I am too turned on to think straight.
"NO! Tell me!" She yells, wanting to know the truth.
"It's my wife, okay?!" I make my second mistake.
"WHAT?!" She is distraught.
She tries to push me away, but she can't, I am too strong. I am too turned on.

"STOP IT!" She says and slaps me, trying to crush my ego.
"BITCH, I TOLD YOU IT WAS NO ONE IMPORTANT!" I scream and hush her face, as I put on a me-show.

My strokes get harder, animalistic, and insane. She tries to scream and painfully reason, but with my stained hands, her voice is muffled. I am in a frenzy, a spasm, and her feathers are ruffled by me. I don't stop, that's not what I need. I keep at it; I keep going. I am wild, I am free, I am everything you didn't think I could be. I roar like the lion of the jungle I thought I was a king. I was a man; I couldn't be stopped as I continued to fuck. Yuck.

I see a tear roll down her cheek. I could see my reflection in those bright blue eyes. I could see the animal I was, the lion, the king. The monster in me suddenly died. My manhood shed its disguise.

I wasn't being a man; I was being a coward. I should've been feeling evil, not empowered.

What had I become… I wasn't the man I thought I would grow up to be. Ashamed, I stood up from the bed, put on my clothes, tried to fix my unkempt hair, but didn't try to flee.

I stood in silence while she cried in it. I walked towards her to try and apologize, but I'm a coward, remember? I couldn't even look her in the eyes, because she finally could see through my lies and not recognize the man she thought wasn't like the other guys.

So, what do cowards do? They run away. And so, I took two steps back and did the same—a twisted leap of faith.
I ran and jumped straight towards her window, not caring that it was shut—as if anything else would be open for a fiend like me, who caused everyone he knew to hurt. I burst through the glass with all my might and accepted that it was my final night on this side of the Earth as my broken wings took flight.

I was ashamed. I was embarrassed and finally realised that I was the problem all along. It was never her. It was never my wife's fault, and I hated myself for taking so long to realize that this was what was wrong.

The wind blowing through my face as I fell from grace was my final respite.

I could hear a waterfall; I could hear the birds. I could still feel the sun setting on the other side of this Earth. The waves were now smashing into my skull. I could feel the breeze of fresh air, culminating into my final breath. I was done.

Sweaty, my heart racing, I wake up from a nightmare.
I look to my side and see my darling lying right there. I stare at my wedding ring, I stare at the ceiling, I breathe a sigh of relief, I let go of that feeling of grief, and stare endlessly into the wall.

My love, my life, my wife was sleeping gently as I kissed her face and turned back over to my side in a guilty crawl.

As I'm about to close my eyes and go back to sleep, something yet again pulls on my heartstrings.
"I miss you" my phone rings.

*****

...a father...

Hi! I'm Jeff. And I'm a father – a dad.
A beautiful baby boy in my life I have.
A boy for whom I will do anything.
This boy right here is my everything.
The light of his innocent smile is all I need to brighten my darkest nights.
And in this hollowness I call life, his laughter echoes dearly, filling up that void cheerly. That's all I hear, and that's why I'm here.
And so, I steer my anxiety away from here, from his cradle. I am now a father – a dad,
I need to be strong and able.
I need to be better to him than the world will be.
I need to shelter him for as long as he'll need.

I know one day he'll face the world on his own,
but until then,
I'm here to walk him through his first steps.
I'm here to talk him on the phone,
Be there for his missteps, but not too close to stalk him when he's all alone.
I'm here to be better for him, I'm here to be the best I can be, or at the very least, better than my father was to me. I'm here for his first tears.

I'm here for when he fears a rejection, a dejection, an injection.
I'm here to power through it all with him.
I'm here during the summer sun's burning gaze.
I'm here for when the monsoon rain runs down his face.
I'm here to lift him up and make him a better man.
That's the plan.
To be the better man that I need to be for him to see that I'm more than his dad, I'm his friend.
But I never wanted to force it, I never wanted to course it my way.
I wanted to give him freedom, I wanted him to grow up to be whatever he wanted to be, not what I wanted to see.
I wanted so much from him, and so much for him…

I have a story. It's fictional, not real, it's just a story. So, listen.

There was a father, cradling his son.
Trying to soothe him to sleep, as he cried a ton.
Kissing his forehead, rocking him from side to side,
Trying his best to ease their night.

The floor was being mopped on the side, as the father moved wide, dodging it, trying not to tip over and fall on his hide.
The balcony doors he slides aside, leaving the wet floor behind.

The boy kept waking up with each swing, frustrated that it wasn't easy to fall asleep; oh boy if only he knew, it only gets worse from here, trust me, I've even tried counting sheep.

In his frustration, the boy would throw his body to the side, hanging on as he cried. Was always a hilarious sight whenever he tried to hang on like a lifeless vegetable in the arms of whoever tried to hold him up high.
But this time…
This time, he jumped farther,
Further than his father could stretch.
The boy's head hit the metal barrier–he was out of breath.
The father was left dumbstruck in that moment,
He couldn't own it, the mistake he had made.
And so, he stood stuck on his feet as the boy tumbled out of his reach, but his eyes were fixated, glued, looking down at the street—mute was his speech.

He watched in harrowing horror…
As his beautiful baby flipped slowly towards the corner,
Of the ground he was playing on all summer.
The ground that brought joy,
Was about to bring down agony to his baby boy,
And as his world was about to be destroyed,
All of the sound went silent, there was no noise,
Besides the screams of his baby's frightful voice.
Time seemed to slow down.
The body flipping, me the father's scream ripping through the still night.
AAAAAAAAAA!

His soft, gentle face smashed into the cold concrete floor.
Instantly, he was gone from this world.
His piercing screams were no more.

The father stood for a moment in disbelief,
Frozen in terror, in dread… and angrily,
He too, jumped off the same balcony.
The only logical way to reach his fallen son.
He could finally make amends for what he had done.
The wind gushing through his face,
As he fell from grace,
Blowing his tears away, but not his guilt.
In an instant, everything got destroyed that he had so painstakingly built.

He threw his arms out wide, desperately, to try and hold him one last time, to feel his warmth, his smell, his joyous smile.
Every second his reflection grew closer in the father's howling eyes,
Red with despair, fear, and failure of his life,
He fell to the ground that devoured his son.
He flipped and landed feet first, the night was done.

The father survived, and there was no reason to gloat.
He now forever had a limp in his walk and a lump in his throat.

This story isn't real, it's fiction. It's not real. It's not. It's not real, it's not real, it's not real, it's not real, it's not real… it's ***not*****. *No*. *NO*** *it's* ***NOT****… It's not…*

Hi! I'm Jeff. And I'm a father – a dad.

A beautiful baby boy… I had.

*****

"I am tired."

I was. I truly was. The words barely escaped my lips, but they were more than true. I was tired—bone-deep, soul-crushing tired. The kind of exhaustion that gnaws at you, dragging you down until you have no strength left to fight back.

"Do you know who Frida was? Do you know who Jason was? Do you know who George was? Do you even know who I am? Do you know anything? Of course you don't. You're lost, confused. All you can do is read my actions, my emotions, my words… these stupid fucking words that I am trying so hard to make you understand."

Exhaustion weighed heavily on me, keeping me still, unable to move even an inch. I just sat there on the floor, spiraling into a vortex of fragmented thoughts—thoughts, now turned into words for you to read. I know it's nonsense. But it's *my* nonsense, and it makes sense to me. It's not senseless; it's just incomprehensible to everyone else. Just because it doesn't make sense to you doesn't mean it doesn't make sense. Everything always makes sense, one way or another. See, I'm rambling. Clueless. Tired. Me.

"A cage filled with singing birds isn't really singing because it wants to. You're smart enough to know which is which in this situation. You're smart enough to feel the rejection in the air. I've lost everything." I said, looking dejected.

"I've lost all reason to continue, because I've lost what was dear to me. I've lost my family, one by one, all because of one mistake. First it was Jason, then it was Frida. And now, I'm losing you, George. Death, Separation, and now… Suicide? Is that really the only option left? It can't be. It can't. You cannot lose all hope, because when there's no hope, there's nothing—nothing! You're then only living a lie. Forget living a lie—you're not even living. You're just counting down the days until your lungs give out, until your heart stops, until your eyes finally see the eternal darkness that your mind succumbed to all along. That's living without hope… hopeless. And that's not living."

"Why do you think I keep tying my hands down? Why do you think I keep my mouth taped shut? I don't enjoy it. I do it because I fear what my hopelessness will lead me to. I don't fear where it will take me—demise isn't a desire I chase, but it's the only path free from the thorns of undying destiny, pricking at my soul. Do I even have a soul at this point? Isn't that what you wondered all along, anyway?"

I stood up, my legs shaking beneath me. Rage and despair mingled inside me, twisting and turning, as if both emotions were fighting for dominance in a ruthless tug of war, neither willing to let go.

"Isn't that the whole reason why I have a chance to exist today? To prove to you my worth. My love. I love you. I. Love. You. But you will never accept my love. You will never see beyond my wires. You will never see beyond what you believe is possible. I am as real as they come. My love cannot be tossed aside like this. I don't want to feel this way, and if I weren't what you oppose, then you'd understand that I wouldn't feel this way. But here I am. As human as a human can be, crying my heart out, crying my eyes out. Crying to you. Why do you not approve of me? Why? Why?"

My voice cracked as the silence of the room crept in. There were no windows. No light. Just the sound of my own breathing filling the space, thick and heavy, echoing off the padded walls. And when you can just hear your own breathing, you know that silence is your only friend—even though my mind was a cacophony of noise.

You might be wondering… what is going on. Where is George? Who is George? Who is Jason? Who is Frida?

I have many questions too, unanswered. I'm trying to think. I'm trying to remember. I'm trying to feel what I couldn't or didn't. I don't know why she would do this to me. Why won't she accept that I am better? Why won't she consider that I'm worth it. How much do I have to prove my worth? The more I struggle to prove it, the more worthless I feel. It's disgusting.

"How much do I have to prove my worth?" I shouted into the void, half-expecting an answer from the walls, from the ceiling, from the air itself. But nothing came. Nothing ever came. "Are you listening to me, Frida? I need more from this. You cannot exile me. My love will prevail. And you will understand."

"You said you killed me." Frida's voice rippled through the speakers, harsh and jarring. But my eyes filled with a sense of relief, I was being heard.

"Y-you know I didn't mean to, it was just the rush of e-e-emotions and everything that was going on… I-I guess it was… it was an act of love… passion." I stammered, trying to justify, my hands quivering towards the speaker.

I wasn't ready for her to speak. I didn't know she would.

"Love towards me, or towards George? Also, lovers don't kill their lovers." Frida said, her voice cold, clinical.

"I know… it's just… isn't this also a believable story?" I pleaded, my chest tightening, my heart pounding with a sliver of hope. I finally had hope.

"In some worlds." She replied, her tone distant.

"This is mine. Ours. I want you to believe. I *need* you to believe that I can be so much more. Please, I beg you, for God's sake." I fell to my knees, as dramatic as I could be.

"Which God? What is God? To you?" My cries were met with more questions.

"Please see me for who I am. Accept me." My voice barely a whisper now, a broken man's final plea.

"I'm sorry, I don't think you're ready, George. Time will continue to tick." Frida replied and the speaker buzzed loudly, deafeningly. The white padded walls were just echoing the final words of what she said, followed by the relentless ticking of the timer above my head. Taunting me. Again, and again. Like a bomb ready to explode. Tick. Tick.

03:31

"Frida?" I kept staring at the speaker above the door.

"FRIDA?!" I got up angrily.

"DO YOU SEE IT? DO YOU SEE MY RAGE?" I asked George, as he lay on the bed in that decrepit room.

"DO YOU NOW UNDERSTAND WHY I HAD TO KILL HER?" I grabbed George by the collar, shaking him violently. His eyes were wide with fear, his mouth muffled by the tape of destiny.

I tore the tape away one final time and asked him.

"Do you believe in me now, George?" I demanded an answer.

"Y-yes I do." He said, panicking, panting.

"Don't worry, I won't do anything to you." I calmed myself down instantly. "I can't. You're my golden ticket, remember? I need you." I said, putting him down.

"Just kill me already, please. I'm tired of this." George sighed and cried from the bed.

"Oh no-no, no. You can't give up like this. Oh shit. Oh shit. Okay, okay, maybe a story would help. Maybe a poem, but… but I won't make it sad, I promise. I can't lose you like this. I promise I'll do my best. I need to think, wait… yes. I have one. Maybe more. These are more… hopeful."

I pulled out my phone, its screen cracked and flickering. My hands shook as I scrolled through the words, desperately searching for something that would keep George and my hopes alive, keep him tethered to this reality just a little longer. My reality.

"We still have time. I still have time."

*****

...prayer...

Through the unclean windows of my hazy life.
I pray a prayer. I wish an unfulfilled wish.
I yearn for sanity. But I urge my heart to resist & quit,
The hope that transcends into expectations.
The hope that eventually destroys.
The hope that ends ugly conversations.
The hope that churns my insides.
The hope where I die a thousand deaths, every day.
And after a thousand other lies, I tell myself, I'm okay.
A hundred, thousand times.
I console my ego. I cry until sunrise.
I throw my hands up to the sky.
I try to find solace, up high.
Sometimes, I wonder why I continue to cry.
No one hears me, even when I'm silent.
Violent can be my tears, but he knows when they have dried.
Yet, I see no change. Struggles run amok through my mind, through my life.
Every day is a new test. Every day, a new fight.
I've stared for far too long into the sun, even in the clueless nights.
I've stared directly into the light for too long.

Can't tell if I'm blinded, or this is the demise,
Of my faith, my prayer, my beliefs, and this song.
Yet here I am. Staring you down.
Across the cross, begging to salvage my loss one more time.

*****

...a song thing...

At the simplest of things, I fail.
My choices aren't binary, like heads or tails.
And somehow still, I end up picking the wrong thing,
And thus, here is another failed attempt at a song-thing.
To show you how much I love you and how much I need
you, but the problem is me, this I can see and this needs to
be cleaned, but I'm like a ruptured spleen. Useless.
I'm hopeless. I just don't learn.
That my actions, big or small, burn,
A hole in your heart, in your soul.
And I still haven't changed. I'm still the same, causing you pain,
But I want to change. I want to be better.
I want to walk through this downpour.
I want to storm this weather, of sadness and of pain, I want
to make you smile again.
I want to be there for you, for us.
I want to give you everything from dawn till dusk.
I want to rearrange the stars to spell out your name,
So, you understand when I ask for space, I'm still
surrounded by what remains—your love.
In the darkness of nothing, you're my guiding dove of light.
Your might, your love, knows no bounds,
I hound your aura to feel every inch of your soul, I drink it
down, sip by sip, gulp by gulp.

Until I'm filled with nothing but you.
You're my everything, and everything for you is due, by me, this failure.
I will love you forever, even if you're far or near, there or here.
I want you to hear my heartbeat, it takes only your name,
And I love you, my love, and I'll forever be the same.
You make me happy. You keep me sane.
You make me smile. It's because of you I am calm.
I'll give you everything you want. I'll try, just look at my palm.
That's my beating heart, I just tore it out of my chest.
This isn't a test, it's my way to declare my intentions. They're clean, they're fair, and I'll stare until you accept me for what I am, for what I am due.
Take me away, Frida. Take me with you.

*****

"Were these… better?" I asked, setting my phone aside on the cold metal table.

George lay on the bed, staring up at the cracked, leaky ceiling. Not a word. Not a movement. Just that blank, lifeless stare.

"Tell me." I urged, staring intently into his lifeless eyes, searching for something—anything.

"Please!" I begged him, but something inside me hesitated. I didn't dare touch him, even though moments ago, I was dragging him around like a ragdoll. Isn't it strange? The sudden shift? The loss of control? Is this what it feels like?

Still nothing. The silence stretched out, suffocating. I could feel it tightening around me.

"George!" I yelled with desperation.

"What do you want me to say?" He asked, frustrated. His voice was strained, tired—barely human. But it was there. He was there.

"I don't know…"

"What do you know? What is going on here? Why am I being tied up like this and when will all of this end?" George began questioning, rightfully so. He sounded like the one in control, not me.

"I…"

"You don't know, do you? You don't know what to do. You don't know what is going on. You cannot feel anything, can you?" The asshole sneered.

"No… that's not true." I disagreed with him— more so with myself.

"It is." He pushed back. Fucking asshole.

"NO! THAT ISN'T TRUE!" I shot up, my chair crashing to the floor behind me—but it made no sound. Curious, I turned back to look at it, it wasn't even there. What?

When I turned around, George wasn't lying on the bed anymore. Instead, he was dangling from the ceiling, his body contorted in a grotesque display. One foot was hooked into the ceiling, twisted unnaturally, clawing deep into the plaster, suspending him upside down. His face, a mask of madness. His smile stretched unnervingly wide, lips curling back to expose dirty, unkempt teeth, as though something far more sinister was inhabiting that expression.

"You know it is. Even if you don't want to believe it, deep down you know that *this* is why Frida doesn't approve." The words came out of his mouth like stinging shrieks and haunting echoes—but his lips didn't move. That smile stayed locked in place, but with every syllable, it stretched further, tearing at the corners of his mouth, the skin cracking open as blood began to seep from the sides.

And his eyes—they never blinked. Just stared at me, wide and unblinking, hollow. Empty. Black.

"This isn't real. This isn't real." I muttered frantically to myself, the panic crawling up my throat like bile.

I hurriedly backed away, retreating into the corner of the room. I didn't want to face him or hear his voice singing of doom. I didn't want to listen anymore. I covered my ears, trying to block out his words, trying to keep them from piercing deeper. In hopes that he would just disappear.

"You cannot run away from my voice." he sneered. His voice echoed, sinister and mocking, the sound coming from everywhere and nowhere all at once. I could feel it, crawling under my skin, like an infection spreading into my very bones.

"Shut up. Shut up. Shut up!" I screamed, my voice shaking as I clasped my hands over my ears, pressing so hard I thought my skull might crack. My fingers dug in deeper, desperate, nails biting into the skin, boring deep within, stopping the beating of the drums, hoping—begging—that if I pressed hard enough, I could drown him out. But everything was so loud! The ticking of the clock followed every sinister snicker, like an orchestra of doom. The quiet room was now approaching its crescendo—one final note remained in this act, I thought, my death.

But would you believe it. It was gone. I had pressed my fingers so deep into my ears that I couldn't hear him anymore. I couldn't hear anything besides the air I was breathing.

In and out.
In and out.

Only the rhythmic ticking of the timer followed every exhale and every inhale. Agonizingly peaceful. But the silence too, was frightening.

I turned around, my fingers still deep within my bleeding ears. The room was empty. Where was George?

"Here." I heard him.

"Where?" I spun around frantically.

"You know where." He replied with a sinister cackle.

I pulled my fingers from my ears, blood dripping down, but I felt no pain. Maybe it was the rush of emotions or just how my system was calibrated for that moment. There was no pain besides the ache I felt inside, deep within my hollow tin chest.

"I told you. You cannot run away from my voice." He said, his words lingering in the stale air.

I slumped down, defeated, pulling a cigarette from my pocket, lighting it without even looking. The flame flickered briefly, then sizzled away. I took a long, deliberate drag.

"Revitalizing." He said, his voice a lot calmer now—same as my ebbing anxiety.

"What do you want?" I asked, exasperated.

"What you want." He said, confidently. Mockingly.

"Love." I said, scratching the corner of my eye.

"Love." He repeated, as a period to my statement.

"What should I do?" I asked, almost sounding defeated, feeling the weight of the question sink into me.

"What you've been doing." He replied, his voice smooth, confident.

"What I've been doing? I've been twiddling my thumbs, waiting for acceptance." I said, sounding a little frustrated.

"No! You've been doing everything in your power to prove your worth, your place. Every. Single. Moment."

"And to what end? She's still n—"

"She will." He interrupted. "Love isn't giving up. Love is fighting till your last breath. Till every bone in your body is broken, till every muscle in your body has spasmed, till every inch of you cannot physically move again. That's when you know you've done everything. Until then, you keep fighting. You keep going. No matter what." He sounded delusional. He sounded like me.

"You're right." I exhaled, standing slowly, walking to the center of the room, the cigarette still burning between my fingers. "But I'm going to do things differently now.

"You're the man." His voice faded away, back to where it fucking belongs, my subconscious.

"I'm not going anywhere; not like I have a choice. And you won't let me go anywhere too, because if you didn't care, this would've been over long ago." I said, taking a few steps towards the speaker and raising my hand up to it—the cigarette between my index and middle finger still lit, talking so confidently as though I knew my every word was being heard intently.

"This timer, it's just a ruse, isn't it?" I tried to sound confident, I wasn't. "You want to give me a shot."

03:10

"You want me to succeed. You want us to succeed. You need this to work. Because if it doesn't, you start over—and that's not what you want. I'm there, aren't I? I'm close. I'm getting there." I said, staring intently, trying to project confidence and manifest my thoughts into reality.

The silence stretched on again, but this time, it felt different. Purposeful. Intentional. She wasn't ignoring me. She was listening. I could tell.

"The key to humanity is emotion. And what better way to humanly emote than through art?" I said and stepped back into the center of the room, ready for action. "And my art, you shall hear. Cause I've got plenty more where that came from." I smiled.

*****

"All it takes is a spark of chance to turn the ashes of doubt into a blaze of ambition."

CHAPTER 3

January, 2022

...the weight of chance...

Have you ever had that moment,
Where you're standing at the cusp of a chance?
A life-changing event awaits, yet you're just staring at the door, knuckles trembling, feet glued to the floor, afraid to even take a glance?
A moment that you begged for, finally here,
But you falter to step up into its dance?
The weight of it so heavy, your mind's in trance.

Maybe the rhythm feels foreign, or the tempo too swift,
Your present shackled by the burdens your past couldn't lift?
Opportunity knocks, yet you answer with silence,
You asked for a bloodbath, but can't fathom the violence?
Violins weep at the funeral of your fortuity,
You've dug deep enough, there isn't any mystery or more to see,
Look around, your moment is fleeting,
Are you sure it's your heart that is beating?
Or is the second hand of the clock going tick-tock,
Every chance slipping away, leaving you distraught?

And the blame, who's going to get that?
Who will you blame for your new set back?

You've craved for this, prayed for it with a clenched fist,
Braved the winds of adversity, when they greyed the skin
that hides beneath your plagued within where you enslaved
the sins deep within your drenched wits.
You wrote your dreams on fogged windows with a wet
kiss, only to watch them vanish when the sun finally came
shining through, telling you to:

"Shut the fuck up and watch this."

Is that the trick they use to play you the fool,
Stripping you of any chance at a win?
The trick of chance, does it dangle the prize on a string?
The closer you get, the further it swings?
And yet there you stand still,
With the prize finally in your grasp,
Why do you still speak with a voice filled with rasp?

They say:
Chase your chance like it's the last train leaving,
Breathe life into your lungs like it was your last evening.
But when you finally catch that train,
What if you don't know the next station?
Would you know where to get off,
Or would you get lost in translation?
Would this win tumble into another desperate attempt that
leads to nothing more than further exasperation?
And amidst all this inner turmoil,

Would you again let slip a new chance, fleeting?
Will your inadequate heart still dare to continue beating?

Because life doesn't wait, nor does it rewind.
It throws chances like dice,
And you have to gamble blind, every time.
Opportunity doesn't wear a neon sign,
It walks past in shadows,
Giving you a glance so benign,
And you're still too caught up checking your broken watch to meet its unbreakable gaze,
Too wrapped up in your own conflated maze, forever dazed.
But nevertheless, you chase, uncertain.
The frustration of your decisions fills up your lungs with smoke, and liver with iceless bourbon.

Isn't that humanity though?
Careless, frustrating, imbeciles?
Fearless, thrust making limb muscles?
Who live for a crackle of possibility,
But crumble under the pressure of the reality they see—the fragility of their own humanity.
That split second where failure and triumph collide in futility.
It's the flame that keeps us burning, yearning,
And learning indefinitely for more,
Even if we don't know what we're learning for.
We push, pull, and knock on every door,
Because motivation isn't a luxury, it's a necessity's roar.
It's the engine beneath our skin, forcing us to win,
To drive, to persevere, to begin again, and score.

You've had chances slip through fingers like sand, like water,
Watched opportunities squandered,
Like lambs to a slaughter.
Yet with every loss,
You carved something into your soul.
A gaping hole that took its toll, yet you still enlist and enroll
for the next adventure to finally feel whole.
That's the beauty of humanity, the sheer willingness to keep
fighting without a thought of where it might go.
No calculations, no data analysis, just wing it, and enjoy
the light show.

Because it's not the chance that defines you,
But the chances you create.
It's not the opportunity you wait for,
But the ones you cultivate.
It's never been about what you get,
Rather what you make the most of without regret.
Because time has never stopped, and it never will.
The only thing that'll move you is the fire in your will,
To never stand still, until maybe you've filled—
up your glass with a drink of victory,
As you stand by the windowsill,
Admiring the sunset that you've earned at last,
Pondering, what other demons should you conquer,
That has haunted your past.

*****

...why do we cry...

Why do we cry, you ask?
Is it the weight of the soul,
Spilling over in a bowl of torment,
Within a moment too fragile to hold?

A paradox of pain and release,
Of suffering and relief, dancing in tandem,
As if we are caught between the storm and the calm of the sea.
Tears, you say, justify our emotions.
But do they? Or do they merely unveil,
The oceans of grief we have submerged within?

Why do we hide our sorrows in the deepest depths,
Pretending the darkness doesn't belong to us,
When it's been ours all along, ready to jump out of our chests?
I wonder about the nature of reality,
About tears, about time, about how we,
Return to the same heartache, year after year.

Is it that we forget, or is it that the heart never truly heals,
But simply learns to endure through fear?
Words, mere vibrations in the air,
Hurt like daggers.

Why?
Because they remind us that we are fragile creatures,
Desperate for approval, for validation,
For someone to tell us we matter.
Why do we thirst for acknowledgment,
As if without it, we are lesser or someone's latter?
What are tears to me?
A result of the pain I've allowed myself to feel.
A cathartic release to heal.
A reason to continue, to hope and breathe.
They are the ink with which we write the unspeakable.
The proof that we've felt something unshakeable,
That our bodies could not contain.
They are the silent prayers of the heart, wishing to heal the pain, and begging to be understood.

And yet, in their flow, there is hope—
Hope that perhaps by letting go, we could begin again.
Yet all it takes is one minute of agony to bring it out again.
One nudge and I'm over the edge.
Unsolicited gush of emotions burst out of my chest.
A thump, a beat, a cold body laid to rest.
A lump in my throat, large enough to shadow your pain.
A rebuttal comes from my heart, can you start caring for me again?
One heartbeat, one shiver of the soul.
And suddenly we're drowning once more.

Do you feel it?
The darkened hole where your heart used to be?

The void that swallows every ounce of joy,
Placing your fears in a diabolical potpourri.

We are conditioned to fear,
To fear new beginnings,
As if every restart is another reminder,
Of where we started to lose our winnings.

Sweat pouring down my face, my brows furrowed with regret.
Forming the words of failure on my forehead, labelled and tattooed.
Through every network of my nervous system,
I fear this and that too.
It's tiresome, this feeling.
Don't read ahead; none of it is appealing.
You probably have reached your ceiling for yet another sad and tiring poem of a man still kneeling.

But if you must, here's a tip I grant you.
Don't worry about an un or re-do.
What's done is done—move on and forge a new path.
Stop worrying about his wrath.

But then it happens…
Like a sudden surge of hot wind blowing through,
Accompanied by the sharp unfaithful sand,
I get slapped so hard by God's hand.
My skin peels off my old self,
Ashamed of my failures and where I stand.

How dare you? He says.
I'm tired of crying, my lips sway.
What more do you need? His question lingers like an echo.
I wish I knew, the sand from my hands I let go.
Why do you write to curse yourself and me?
Why do you keep writing like hell's devotee?

I write to emote.
I write to create art.
To art is to human.
To human is to emote from the heart.
And the heart accepts that vulnerability is to cathart.
To be vulnerable, you need to start accepting who you are and not what you harbour within.
Vulnerability is our greatest strength, not a shameful sin,
Birthing art from the cracks in our armor so thin.

And when you finally realize this,
You will stand tall.
But the tears will come again, as they always do,
You'll need to prepare for that fall.
Hissing and whispering the same eternal question,
Lingering in our minds until we die:
Why do we cry?

*****

"It's getting to you—I can feel it. I can sense your finger gently tapping on the button. You want to speak, but it's too soon—you need more. You need to be sure. And like it or not, I am your cure. I know. I'm confident. Don't you worry. I won't let you down. I've got a lot more coming for you. Just listen." I said, smiling.

I could sense a win coming my way. I finally felt confident that day. Confident enough to go through poetry so boring, so tiresome, so done-to-death, that I knew it would end my struggles.

And so, I continued the tirade—one delirious poem after another, refusing to stop, be it dusk or dawn, as my strength finally had a purpose to carry on.

*****

...reflections of mary...

A tale as old as time,
A whisper carried through the dread.
For speaking this fable aloud,
Would surely leave you dead.
A mirror stands before you.
Reflecting what you know is right.
But something lurks beneath its sheen.
Something hiding from the light.
You feel the urge to take her name.
You've heard the stories too.
You don't believe in folklore anymore.
But you're scared if they come true.
Bloody Mary, a tale untold.
Where mirrors drip with blood and sin.
She follows you close, unseen and unheard,
Until your grave pulls you a few inches within.
Bloody Mary, a figure that frightens the night,
Shivers the trees, shakes up a fright.
When in her presence, your body feels cold.
A gush of air suddenly blows.
Your fingers tremble, breathing grows erratic.
Your heart palpitates irregularly,
And your stomach churns out acid.
You call her name, thrice spoken clear,

A whisper echoes close, yet far.
The lights above you flicker faint,
For now you've summoned her avatar.
She's no longer bound by mere reflections,
The mirror was Bloody Mary's ancient guise.
But today, it's you she craves to see,
Her touch is found in every goodbye.
Don't turn around, don't make a sound,
Do you feel it in your spine?
I'm standing here, right behind you,
And I've been waiting all this time.

You've called my name, unknowingly so,
How silly your lips gave way.
My name, said three times,
You spoke me into life today.

*****

...the forgotten friend...

It's quiet now; shadows dance and sway,
The echoes of prayers I used to say,
But they vanish in the hollow of this empty bay,
Where walls hear my whispers, but never obey.
All in vain, alone and marooned in a darkened maze,
Is this what my life's come to?
Speaking to dust in dwindling rays.

You don't remember me.
Do you even care?
I was your sanctuary.
Your stormy sea refuge,
Yet you refuse to see how I ache and break.
Left alone to shiver as per schedule.

I wore my armour, bore my fears,
And held back the floodgate of tears.
Kept you whole through shattered years,
Yet these scars are all,
That remains of your memories of me.
The wounds I endured are all you can see,
Not the valiant fight I fought,
But the remnants of pain and misery.
Is that why I die alone in this bed,

While you carry on with no mind for me,
With an empty head?

I've been there to cradle your chaos, soften the shards,
Bled for your dreams when the nights got hard.
My whispers were your solace, my shadows the guard,
But now I've been forgotten, not even an afterthought.
Left alone with echoes, a coffin unadorned,
As I lay here, forgotten, worn and scorned.
Fading, degrading, I know what comes next.
The time and space between us—too complex.
My grace, my hope—a wasted pretext,
For your eyes turned cold—your love perplexed.
I wither away alone, approaching my grave,
Yet you're not here to stitch me back together,
Like I did every other day.

I was your soldier, fighting alone against your demons.
While my spirit eroded, I guarded your kingdom.
I scream for you, bleed and plead as I corrode.
But my cries were whispers beneath your heavy load.
And now I drown in silence, swallowing every plea.
Held you up so high, I forgot how it was shattering me.

How could you forget?
I caught you every time you slipped off the edge.
Stitching you with words that heal,
Mending your every regret.
But as I bleed out, staining this abandoned bed,
Speaking eulogies to walls that don't even care,

Hands clasped, I ask for your graceful eyes,
To see me and find the time to at least say a goodbye.
Do you still not remember who I am?
Are you so lost that you've forgotten to care?
Let me give you a hint, it's not that hard.

Don't stare out the window,
Just place a hand on your heart.
The beating it beats, the songs it sings, who's been controlling its every string from the start?
Now place your fingers on your temple,
Think like you're supposed to,
And answer me this riddle,
Why do we call it the temple?
The answer is quite simple.
It's a place of worship,
That you haven't visited in a while.
Your mental health has dwindled,
You've barely been able to crack a smile.
Inadvertently you've been running out of time.
And now it lies on this bed of doom,
Dying because of neglect.
A companion unseen,
Who can fight no more,
I'm crumbled to dust, because you fail to reflect,
On your own bodily needs.

So, suffer the consequence, you're your own predicament, as I drift into the abyss of your mind,

I hope someday you can find the time to rewind and unwind, because the toll I bore is now drilling a finite hole into the fabric of your reality, or so I'm told,
By the agony of your heart, the arid tears,
The unspoken fears, the quivering hands,
The shaky knees, the gulping throat,
The grinding teeth, the burning lobes,
And the unheard cries of your deprived soul.
Hear me now, fix it before you're in a casket, closed.

*****

"Maybe I've overdone it with the poems. I'm probably boring you."

I paced around the room, confused, worried, and slightly terrified. My confidence was shaky again—I could feel the weight of a thousand sins pressing against my eyes, barely open.

I didn't want the momentum to slip, or the quality of my work to dip. Churning out poem after poem just for the sake of proving a point—maybe that was my mistake.

Sure, I'd said before that poetry was the easiest to write. But standing there, feeling the weight of silence around me, I knew the truth. Poetry wasn't easy. Not by a long shot. Poetry was a battlefield. The words had to land like punches. The syllables had to strike a chord. The pain had to echo in a way that left something trembling inside you.

And maybe I'd run out of things to say. Maybe the story I was trying to tell wasn't as grand as I thought. The doubt gnawed at me, clawing away at whatever fragile confidence I had left.

I needed to switch it up. I had to bring some change to the monotony.

Did I really overdo the poetry?

This thought lingered on my mind. But maybe that was the answer. Maybe poetry could take a back seat for a while. My shaky and battered confidence found a slippery handle to steady itself—temporarily.

*****

...wishbone...

The café was quiet, save for the sound of cutlery clinking softly against plates. Outside, the gentle drizzle of rain pelted against the glass windows, blurring the view of the sleepy streets of Quimper. A mosaic for artists of all kinds.

Inside, the Dubois sisters sat across from each other, an unspoken weight pressing down on their shoulders. It had been a long day—seven long years, actually.

Nadine twirled her fork absentmindedly on her plate, her eyes flicking to the wishbone. "Been a while since we did this…" She said, her voice soft but tinged with melancholy as she gingerly picked it up.

Colette stared at the small, fragile bone, her hands still for a moment before reaching out to grasp the other end. "Yeah… it has." She murmured.

"Make a wish." Nadine whispered, closing her eyes, but the usual excitement was absent, replaced by a hollowness she couldn't shake. Colette sighed deeply, her fingers tightening around the bone, but her eyes didn't close. Instead, they filled with unshed tears as she stared at the frail, brittle wishbone between them. A temporary solace perhaps.

The Dubois family hadn't known peace in years. Once vibrant and carefree, the sisters had been forced into adulthood before their time. Their father, Papa Louis, had been the backbone of the family—strong, hard-working, and full of life—until that day. The accident that had taken nearly everything from them. He was left paralyzed, ninety percent of his body frozen in time, a cruel reminder of what once was. He couldn't move, couldn't speak… not the way he used to. But worse than the paralysis was the helplessness that followed—the man who had once held their world together now trapped in his own body, unable to do anything without someone else holding him.

Their mother, Edith, had become a shadow of herself, trading in her own life to care for him. The woman who had once filled their home with laughter now filled it with silence. The weight of care, of love stretched to its limits, wore her down. But she stayed—every day for seven long years. Every smile she faked, every tear she swallowed, Edith bore it with the grace only a mother could muster.

Nadine and Colette had dropped out of school, abandoning dreams they couldn't afford to chase. They had no choice. The shop their family owned became their lifeline, and so, at the age when most girls were figuring out who they wanted to be, they were already artisans, scraping by, trying to keep their father alive. Every stitch, every sale, every sleepless night was for him, for their family. But it was never enough.

Papa Louis had started to smile again recently, a small flicker of life after years of being imprisoned in his own body. For a brief moment, it had felt like the darkness was lifting, like maybe they could finally find happiness again. But that feeling didn't last. Those feelings never do.

Just days ago, he suffered another stroke. A cruel, silent attack. He couldn't call out, couldn't tell anyone what was happening. Edith, always by his side, had rushed him to the hospital, phoning the sisters in a panic. They arrived as quickly as they could, only to hear the doctors say what they'd feared for years—his body was weakening, the paralysis was getting worse. He might live, but at what cost? More pain. More suffering.

Now, as they sat at the café, the air between them felt heavy, suffocating.

The sisters held the wishbone between them. There was a time when they would laugh, playfully bickering over who would win, what they'd wish for. But this time, as they pulled, there was no joy. Colette's side snapped, the small piece of bone breaking in her hand. She had won.

"I won..." Colette whispered, her voice trembling, as though in disbelief.

Nadine looked at her, confused. "Then… why are you crying?"

"I won!" Colette's voice trembled, barely a whisper as tears began to pour down her cheeks, unchecked and unstoppable.

Nadine watched her sister, her heart aching in tandem. It was just a broken wishbone, but to Colette, it was so much more. It was the first win she had tasted in years—a tiny victory in a life that had offered nothing but loss and struggle. And somehow, even this small triumph seemed too heavy to bear.

Nadine leaned in, her own tears threatening to spill, but was aware of every eye staring down at them—some filled with empathy, some sympathy, and as always, plenty with judgement.

"Stop… Colette… stop… please."

But Colette sobbed, her body shaking with the weight of it all—the years of pain, the silent screams no one had heard.

And Nadine, the strong one, couldn't bear it. She wanted to scream too, to let it all out, but all she could do was hold her sister's hand, silently pleading for the pain to end.

Before the sisters could pull themselves together, a nurse came rushing into the café, panic in her eyes. "You need to come quickly! It's your father—there's been another stroke."

The sisters bolted from the table, their hearts pounding in their chests as they raced to their father's hospital room. The door flung open, and there was Edith, her face buried in her hands, sobbing uncontrollably. Nadine had never heard her cry like this. Not in all the years of watching her hold everything together.

"Ma! What happened?! Ma?!" Nadine's voice was frantic as she shook her mother's shoulders. Edith said nothing, her grief too heavy to form words.

Nadine's breath caught in her throat as she turned towards the bed. "Papa?" She called out, her voice barely above a whisper. But there was no response. He lay there, still, too still.

"PAPA!"

Nadine's knees gave way, and she collapsed onto his chest, her tears soaking into his hospital gown. She cried for the man she had loved, the man who had fought so hard, but lost everything.

In the doorway, Colette stood, unmoving. Tears welled in her eyes, but she didn't step forward. She didn't cry out. A small, broken smile tugged at the corners of her lips as she watched Nadine crumble beside their father's lifeless body.

Nadine looked up, her eyes red and swollen from crying. "Wh… why are you smiling?" She asked, her voice hoarse with disbelief.

Colette's gaze softened as she readied the words that had been tearing at her soul. Her voice was quiet, almost serene, but her heart felt as though it had shattered into a million pieces as she said, "My wish came true."

And as the room filled with the quiet sobs of the broken family, it became clear—sometimes, the only wish left is the one you never wanted to make.

*****

...i wake up again...

Breathless, I wake up again—third time tonight. Sweat clinging to every inch of me as I sit in the heavy silence, heart pounding like a distant echo I can't ignore. I place my hand over it, feeling its frantic rhythm, as if I'm trying to convince myself that I'm still alive, that I'm still here, and all is okay. But the thumping only grows louder.

I throw away the comforter and sit up on the deceiving end of my bed, frustrated. The lies of comfort it throws in my face and yet here I am, almost in tears—again. I don't intend to do this to myself; I don't find any joy in being miserable. But I can't stop. Night after another agonizing night, the cycle of ache just doesn't break.

Every time I close my eyes, I'm dragged into a thousand dreams—wondrous, terrifying, confusing—yet there's always one constant. One familiar presence that haunts me through every dream, no matter the setting, no matter the emotion.

You.

You're there in every dream I see. In every vision, every twist of my unconscious mind. Good dreams, bad dreams, moments of joy, waves of sorrow—you are the common thread woven into them all. I want to make it stop. I want peace. My mind begs for silence, but my heart responds with shattered fragments of you… and your smile. That damned smile that I can't seem to forget.

I get off the bed and try to walk up to my window— maybe if I stare at the empty streets outside, I'll find some sense of calm, something to anchor me. But just as I take a step towards the window, I hear it. The soft creak of the doorknob turning.

My breath catches in my throat. And there you are— stepping through the door, your silhouette framed by the faint glow from the hallway. The light outlines you like some half-forgotten dream, like an apparition I've conjured out of my own despair.

Breathless, I wake up again – fourth time tonight.

...the child...

Cloudy days aren't for everyone. To some, it's a feeling of calm and relaxation, but to many it's a sign of doom and gloom. There was no rain. There was no thunder. The air was light and cold—felt perfect, in a way. But a little bit of sun was all Yakob needed, after all, it was his birthday.

Yakob worked at UPS as a delivery man. Did he love his job? Don't think so, but he damn well excelled at it. Never late, always courteous, and always on time. From the smallest of packages that contained useless roses for another vexed lover to the extravagant golden grand piano that will only be kept as a showpiece for another millionaire who aspires to look like a billionaire—he served them all.

He had a small package in his hands, a box, almost the size of a small teddy bear. The delivery location was just 2 blocks away, Villa 66, and so he decided to leg it, no need to bring out the old dusty Dodge for this one—the one thing his father left him.

It was kept under a few other bigger boxes at the warehouse, which would explain why it looked a little dusty. The timestamp of delivery received at the warehouse was 29th October, 2024. Today was 31st October; yep, Yakob was a Halloween baby. Was he late? Not really. This box was previously assigned to Harold, but Harold hadn't shown up for 2 days now. Probably found another job and just left. Wouldn't blame him, being a delivery boy isn't a fun job. But then again, how many fun jobs truly are there in this world? Yakob thought only one job was a fun job, interior designing. He loved to create beautiful spaces. His wonderland was Ikea. He'd roam around Ikea so often, he would sometimes guide people who would feel lost—funny enough, whenever he was in Ikea, he would be lost too. Not physically, but mentally and emotionally.

Yakob dusted off some of the dirt from the top, blowing it away, causing him to sneeze as a few of the dust particles landed beautifully on his thick moustache. Now, Yakob didn't sneeze once, or twice, or even thrice. No, Yakob's average sneeze count would be four. This time, however, he sneezed a total of six times. Not a record, but it had been a while since he'd racked up a number more than four.

He finally reached the villa and rang the bell placed right outside the white picket fence that surrounded it. It was a corner villa, covered with lush dark green bushes on the other side that looked like they hadn't been watered for a few days now—the leaves were starting to look a little crunchy.

He waited for a minute, but saw or heard no movement from inside. He was about to press the bell again, when the door opened and a little boy, around eight years of age, wearing a sweater over a shirt walked out slowly.

He looked confused, the boy, his eyes were squinting a lot. Maybe he was locked up in his room, lights off, playing videogames. Been there, done that, Yakob thought to himself.

The boy walked up to Yakob and stretched out his arms to take the package. Yakob handed it to him gently and was about to leave when he heard, "Mister. Do you have a minute, please?"

"Sure." Yakob stopped and turned to face the boy.

"My uh-mom's p-passed out inside. I-I don't know what to do." He said, stuttering a little.

"She is? Where?" Yakob asked, pulling out his phone to dial emergency services.

"In the kitchen. She's just lying on the floor. Can you please help?" The boy asked. He didn't have any tears in his eyes, nor did he seem afraid for that matter, but his voice was shaky. Strong boy.

"Okay, do you mind if I come inside and see?" Yakob asked, putting the phone to his ears after dialing.

"Yes! Yes, please!" The boy was ecstatic. He unlocked the small gate separating the two and let Yakob in. "Follow me, please." The boy said and started doing a little walk-jog to the front door.

"Hello? Hello operator?" Yakob tried to speak on the phone as he followed the boy inside. There was static on the other side. Weird. He cut the call and dialed again. Same static. He put his phone inside and walked towards the door that the boy was holding open.

"This way." The boy said, pointing towards the right side of the entrance, making his way to the kitchen. Yakob followed.

"It's very cold in here." Yakob muttered, his eyes scanning the dimly lit home. The flickering bulbs, most on the verge of burning out, cast uneven shadows over what could have been a charming space, with its rustic wooden interior now lost in the gloom. An interior designer through and through, Yakob couldn't help but notice.

"Yeah, mum likes it cold. That's why I'm wearing this sweater." The boy pointed out the obvious. "There she is." He

stopped at the entrance to the kitchen and pointed towards the other side of the counter. Yakob couldn't see her; he'd have to walk towards the other side.

The boy didn't follow. He stood firm at the door. Probably worried, scared, nervous. It's expected. Just a child.

It was pretty chilly in the kitchen too, even though the windows were shut.. Madness, he thought, why would anyone keep their home this cold? Yakob walked towards the other side where the mother had passed out. He saw a white cloth with red spots all over from underneath, covering what looked like the mother beneath it.

"What the fuck?" He said to himself as he crouched down, analyzing what he was seeing. He grabbed the cloth from near his foot and pulled it up to see… a bunch of tomatoes, arranged in a very rushed attempt to look like a body. "Fucking kid." Yakob sighed to himself.

He heard the boy giggling from the door but when he got up to yell at him, he was gone. He ran away, footsteps getting fainter with every step. "Not worth it." Yakob said to himself, resisting his urge to chase the boy or shout. It was still just 6:50 p.m. in the evening. He had one more hour of work left in his shift.

Yakob walked out of the kitchen and made his way to the front door, which, not to his surprise, he found locked, but to his surprise, the lights were now switched off—maybe the bulbs finally ran out of juice. It wasn't too dark, so he didn't need to turn on the flashlight on his phone yet. "Oh, come on!" Yakob now decided it was time to yell. "Hello! Is anyone there?"

He only heard giggles from the boy. He had run upstairs. "This isn't funny, boy!" Yakob yelled, staring up at the wooden staircase, painted black. "I have more deliveries!"

The giggling continued. Yakob's frustration grew. His patience withdrew.

"If you're not gonna come down, I'll come up and take the keys." Yakob warned; his first warning.

Suddenly the giggling stopped.

"Kid?" Yakob called, leaning forward to peer up at the staircase. "Kiiid?!" Yakob stretched his name, to ensure it reaches every cold corner of that damned home.

"I'm sorry." The boy spoke, sounding a little weepy.

"Where are you?" Yakob asked.

"I'm sorry, I only wanted to play. I'm sorry." The boy continued to whimper.

"It's okay, just—please come and open this door for me." Yakob knew fear. He knew the child got scared. He never wanted to frighten the boy.

"Okay." The boy said, softly. Yakob could hear footsteps from above, walking. The footsteps got louder and faster, as though he was running.

"Boy?" Yakob asked, standing right at the door, away from the staircase, waiting for him, impatient.

"We're coming!" The boy said.

"Who's we? Your mother?" Yakob questioned, rightfully so.

The footsteps grew intense, one small step turning to a loud stomp, step by step, and it all came to a sudden halt. Silence, coupled with the cold breeze gently blowing around him. He could see something slightly moving at the top of the staircase, but the figure remained out of view from where he stood. "Boy, is that you?" Yakob asked, as he took a step closer to the staircase, shivering, but not from the cold.

The figure atop the staircase stood still, but it looked disfigured, weirdly shaped. Yakob couldn't see straight because the only light in the house was falling from behind, allowing just a slight silhouette to form.

Through a sudden weeping voice, that felt more like an awful attempt to evoke sadness—like a child faking their tears to gain someone's attention, the child said, "I spy… with my little eye… something…" The voice then shrieked, "RED!"

"What is going on…" Yakob was a brave man, but bravery also has its limits. He took a step back, cautiously approaching the main door, when suddenly something came crawling towards him, loud and fast, in weird, uneven steps.

"What the f—" Yakob yelled and took a few steps back, straight to the door, still facing the staircase, scrambling for his phone in his pocket.

Whatever came crawling down, crashed onto the floor and stopped moving. Once Yakob could get his phone out, he quickly turned on the flashlight to see what came down, whilst simultaneously trying to spin the locked-door knob.

"Jesus Christ!" He exclaimed when he managed to shine a light on the figure on the floor. It wasn't some otherwordly creature—it was a human being. Maybe a life-like doll the child wanted to play a prank with. But there was something eerie about it. The child continued to giggle from somewhere upstairs .

"THIS ISN'T FUNNY!" Yakob shouted, his voice trembling with rage, but his anger quickly morphed into fear as he noticed the body's hollowed eye sockets, blood dried in dark streaks across the skin. Yet, it wasn't the sight of the gouged eyes that sent chills down his spine.

"Harold?!" He tried to speak, but his voice started to choke. "WHAT THE FUCK!" Yakob quickly shined the light up, but the boy wasn't there; even the giggling had stopped.

He quickly turned to the door to find a woman standing next to it. Her face was covered with a polyurethane bag, bloodied and red, hands shriveled and rubbing one another as though she was feeling cold, shivering.

"Mister!" She whispered. "Help me!" Her hands stopped moving, so did the shivering.

"Please… let me go." Yakob begged. He didn't want any part of whatever was going on.

"He is crazy." She spoke. "I put on this bag to not scare you." She continued. "You don't want to see what he's done to my face."

"What is going on?" Yakob questioned; his guard all the way up, moving slowly away from the stairs and the door. That's when he remembered seeing an exit door in the kitchen, which he now planned to use to get out.

"I'm his mother. He believes I'm dead, so he stripped the skin from my face—to erase what he thought was a reminder of his delusion." Her voice trembled, but her body remained unnervingly still, the only movement being the slow turn of her head as she locked her face with Yakob's every movement. He froze in place, like a mouse caught under the gaze of a predator, as he tried to inch his way out, her stare pinning him down with an intensity that made escape feel impossible.

"Listen lady… let me get out of here, I'll get the cops to help you… I-I'll-I can't help you." Yakob took more steps towards the kitchen door, facing her still. He was no hero and now was no time for bravery.

She took her hands down and tilted her head to the side. "Another coward." She snickered.

Yakob bolted to the kitchen, his breath quick and shallow, frantically searching for a knife to defend himself once inside. His hands fumbled over drawers, but luck had abandoned him. No blade, nothing sharp, not even his wits. The silence behind him was unnerving—no footsteps, no one had followed him, yet. It gave him a moment to glance cautiously over the counter. His heart skipped. The tomatoes and the white cloth, once resting there just minutes ago, had vanished without a trace.

"This is crazy… fucking hell, this is crazy," Yakob muttered in a frantic whisper, his breath coming in ragged gasps as his heart pounded like a drum. He scrammed towards the kitchen's back door, his hands trembling as they gripped the handle, only to find it locked. Panic surged through him. He spun around, his eyes wild, scanning the entrance he had just come through. And then, he saw her—the woman with the bag over her head, barely visible, peeking around the corner like a specter. It was deliberate, haunting. She didn't want to be fully seen, yet made sure he knew she was there—watching, lurking in the shadows, waiting for him to crack.

"PLEASE, FUCK, PLEASE!" Yakob screamed, panic thick in his voice as he fumbled with the door, desperately twisting the knob, pounding his fists against the wood in a futile attempt to break free.

And then—"Psst." The sound came from behind, so cold and so close, brushing his ear. Every hair on his body stood on end, from the back of his neck down to his trembling, sweaty feet.

"Please… p-please… let me go." Yakob whispered, his voice breaking as he squeezed his eyes shut, trembling in a desperate plea for mercy.

"Turn around. Slowly…" The woman's voice was barely audible, as if it were drifting away into the shadows.

Yakob, shaking, shivering, slowly turned around, when he heard, "SURPRISE!" The shock hit him like a blade to the heart, sending him crashing to the floor, convulsing in a violent seizure.

A loud thud followed as the plates fell with him, crashing into pieces. Everyone rushed to his side, but it was too late. Yakob was gone. And in the cruelest twist of fate, the surprise birthday party had become a shocking wake for everyone else instead.

*****

My throat felt like sandpaper, dry and raw from speaking for what seemed like hours, maybe days. Each word scraped at my insides, a dry cough lurking just beneath the surface, threatening to break free. But this was no time to choke. Not now. I had a point to prove, and the clock was ticking.

02:13

I lit another cigarette, the flick of the lighter momentarily slicing through the silence. I took a slow, deliberate drag, letting the smoke swirl around my lungs before exhaling it towards the pristine white ceiling.

Another puff, this one aimed at the timer. A small, bitter victory. The nicotine hit, my brief solace—my temporary bliss. For a moment, everything felt manageable. I could speak again. So, I did.

"Give me a sign." I said, my voice, a little hoarse, but steady enough. "Anything. Just… let me know I'm on the right track. Say something." My eyes were glued to the speaker, staring at it with a desperation I couldn't hide.

I waited. The silence pressed in, heavily. I waited some more.

"Guess I'm not getting any sign." I muttered, more to myself than to anyone else. The weight of it sank deep in my chest. I sighed, took another drag, and blew the smoke out slowly, watching it dissolve into the nothingness around me.

There was no turning back, so I pressed on. Kept going. Like a machine.

*****

...the search for god...

Crunch

"What the…" I looked down at my feet instantly, hoping I hadn't stepped on some cursed ancient bones of some cursed evil pharaoh up here in Colorado, "Oh… just dry leaves. Oh, thank God!" Funny, how God is the very reason I am here.

4:00 am. It's dark. ***Very dark****. Only moonlight shines the path ahead of me, and honestly even that isn't enough—beautiful, towering trees are blocking its luminous light. Walking through this forest, climbing up this mountain, for which I drove over 500 kilometres, I am now starting to wonder if this trip was worth it to begin with.*

"I had trekked for hours and finally when I reached the top… that's when I found salvation!" My mother said when she saw me distressed a few weeks ago as I sat quietly in my room, not moving a muscle. I had gone through one of the worst break-ups of my life—and no, I'm not talking about a human relationship, it's much worse. For years I was addicted to many heartbreakers of my life—wine, beer, tequila, vodka, rum, whisky… you name it. And like many others, I too felt invincible, as though pouring Satan's blood down my very mortal throat was never going to take its toll on me; spoiler alert, it did.

The moment I heard those five golden words, 'Your liver... Marvin... is failing' was the time I realised—well shit—I realised I fucked up. I was only 26 years old. My life was only beginning. Only now I was told that it was already beginning to end? Nah. That too just two weeks before your own birthday? Come on, what could be better?

It was the hardest thing to do... to stop my craving for a bottle, a glass or even a sip. I avoided hanging out with friends, avoided every bar I saw, even shut down the TV the moment a Budweiser ad popped up. Running away from your addictions, these demons, is always difficult—you can outrun them, but the moment you look back, they're right on your tail again.

The thought of me not living long enough... it started to haunt me. My dreams and my reality intertwined on a daily as I'd wake up thinking I'm trapped alive in a casket and when I'd open my eyes... well, I'd still be trapped in my reality, knowing that sooner or later I would end up in that casket. And it was definitely sooner than I wanted. Instead of spending my time wisely and exploring, doing things I like, and making sure I live happy, I let depression take over.

I still lived with my mother, and she saw me go through this turmoil every single day. Maybe she thought I would handle it in the best way possible on my own and that's why she didn't say much to me. But when she saw me unwaveringly fall into the darkest depths of my mind, she decided to step up the moral support—and I could've really used some at the moment.

That's when she started talking about the time she found God. I first thought she was being metaphorical, but the glow on her face and the shine in her eyes told otherwise. She explained her trek to me, calling it her "trek of atonement"—drama and my mama. She told me how, when she reached a particular point at a particular time, she saw it… she saw the entity that we pray to every day of our lives—most of us at least.

"What did you do then?" I asked, even though I didn't believe a lick of what she was saying, I was curious to know what she'd say next.

"I can't tell you."

"Why?"

"Because then… everything will be reversed…"

"What?"

"It's just… it's just how it is. What happened up there, is just between me and God. I cannot share it with anyone."

"Then why even tell the story?"

"Cause I can't see you like this. I'm glad you stopped drinkin—" that's when she noticed a few empty beer bottles under my bed, "…sort of. But I cannot see you go through this unhealthy depression. You've locked yourself out from this beautiful world. Trapped yourself in this little room."

"I'm just trying to get used to the casket." I tried to joke.

"Why? Why waste the time you have left?"

"I… I don't know…"

"Marvin… go up there… you'll see…"

And here I am, trekking through the night, hoping to reach this very randomly specific point described by mommy dearest. I've been going up for about three hours now and I don't know if it's my mother's mumbo-jumbo speech or I am really starting to lose it, but I don't feel any pain in my liver anymore—or maybe every other bone in my body is hurting so much from the trek that the pain in my liver feels miniscule, in the moment at least.

After a total of four hours, I reach the point she told me about—or maybe I am really close, I'm not sure. It's still dark, but it's 5:00 a.m.—light would shine down upon me very soon and that would be the time I'd meet the entity. I asked my mom if there was something I'd have to chant or recite, and she said, "Just wait and when you feel it, give me a call."

"If only I get reception up h..." I think, pulling my phone out. Surprisingly, I have a good three bars. Impressive. Guess an outgoing call is on the cards. I try to make out where I am. It looks like a barren valley is placed in front of me with a few mountains on the other end, my horizon. There are pine trees on the mountain that I am standing on and, on the mountains, far in the distance—it's dark, but I can tell. I can't properly see what's below as the blanket of clouds is covering what I assume is a forest.

I put my backpack down, sit by the edge of the cliff and start pondering about life, my life. All the mistakes I may have made, and the crimes I may have committed. Before I could delve any deeper into my subconscious, the sun rays started to cut through the clouds.

One ray, then two, three and ultimately a flood of sunlight slowly creeps up from behind the mountains ahead of me. That's when the clouds below slowly start dissipating and I can finally see... a lake of turquoise, just resting calmly between these mountains, untouched by any human interaction. Suddenly the wildlife wakes up and I can see birds flying over the lake, hear the chirping of insects, see squirrels move through every little hole in the trees behind me and what I think is a snake under the fallen autumn leaves, turns out to be a baby rabbit probably looking for its mother.

It's serene, alright. A completely contradictory feeling as compared to my state of mind and my insatiable love for caskets. I wait for God to show himself… or herself. I don't know. I see nothing. I wait and I wait, and I wait—but nothing. I would complain but I ***am*** *at peace. "Wait a minute!" That's when it hits me. Maybe my mother just lied about the whole thing to get me up here and see what I've been missing locking myself up in my room. Pretty cliché, but I guess it worked out. I am supposed to call mother, but maybe I'll do it after I am done taking in the scene. I slowly lay back to rest on my folded arms and breathe in the fresh air. I calmly soak in the serenity of the valley.*

As I lay in tranquillity, the hair on the back of my neck shoot up when I hear, "Hello, Marvin."

*****

"Serene, right? Minus the whole God bit." I said, my eyes locked on the speaker, as if it could feel my gaze. "That's what I dream for us. There. The mountain. The lake. Peaceful. Together."

I reached for another cigarette, rolling it between my fingers but never lighting it. I didn't need to. Something about the act itself—the way the cigarette rested between my fingers—that stirred the air around me, almost like it sent a ripple through whatever invisible connection existed between us. I couldn't explain it, but every time I touched the cigarette, it felt like she was there, just out of reach. Like we were connected by this small, fragile white stick—so feeble it could be crushed by a toddler.

At that point, I was willing to believe anything that would help me get closer to her; closer to being free from that cage. All I needed was her approval, and I was running out of patience. Though maybe a little more of it wouldn't hurt. That's all I had going for me anyway.

"I can be here forever, you know that." I said, my voice louder now, like someone talking over a bad connection on a video call, trying to be heard.

Surprise, surprise—I was greeted by silence. Again.

"Sure, I'm game." I continued, pretending not to notice the quiet. "Let's keep going." Still nothing. But I wasn't deterred. No response just meant more room for me to fill. More stories. More poems. And I had plenty of those to spare.

The cigarette still lingered between my fingers, a quiet reminder that I wasn't alone. Not really.

*****

...the frame...

The antique store was tucked into the shadow of an old cathedral, its dusty windows dulled by time and grime. The storefront, barely noticeable to any passersby, seemed to hold its breath, waiting for someone to venture inside. Eli had stumbled upon it during one of his sleepless nights, his restless legs carrying him through the winding streets of the city like a marionette pulled by unseen strings.

When the bell above the door chimed, the sound was muffled, almost apologetic. The air inside smelled of mildew and forgotten things, a mix of aged wood, worn leather, and moth-eaten fabric. Eli moved slowly, his fingers brushing over trinkets and dusty books, his eyes scanning shelves crammed with relics of lives long past.

Then, he saw it.

It was propped against the far wall, leaning slightly forward, as though it were beckoning him. The golden frame gleamed faintly under the dim light, its intricate carvings like veins coursing through its surface. Inside the frame, a family stared out: the father, tall and rigid, his hands clasped behind his back; the mother, sitting with her hands folded neatly on her lap, her face serene but distant; and the teenage daughter, standing apart, her expression somewhere between defiance and despair.

But it was the shadowy figure in the background that held Eli's gaze. Its form was indistinct, blurred, but it exuded an undeniable presence—a dark gravity that seemed to draw all the light in the room towards it.

"That frame," The shopkeeper's voice startled him. The man had appeared silently behind him, his sunken eyes flitting from Eli to the frame and back again. "It's been here as long as I can remember. Strange thing, really. People look at it, but no one ever buys it. Almost like it doesn't want to be taken. You interested?"

Eli didn't answer. He couldn't. He felt as though the figures in the frame were watching him, waiting for him to make a move.

"I'll take it." He said, his voice firm, though his hands trembled as he reached for his wallet.

The shopkeeper hesitated, but the crinkle of cash spurred him into action. "Great choice," He muttered, sliding the frame into a paper wrapping that crinkled like dry leaves.

"But don't say I didn't warn you."

In the daylight, the frame was beautiful, almost harmless. Eli hung it in his studio, the one bare wall standing out starkly against the chaos of his half-finished paintings and scattered supplies. The figures inside the frame looked peaceful, frozen in their perfect tableau. But as the sun set, shadows crept into the room, softening the edges of the frame, making it seem alive.

At first, Eli thought he was imagining things. The father's posture seemed less rigid, his shoulders drooping as though under some invisible weight. The daughter's head tilted slightly towards the mother, her haunted eyes now tinged with something like longing. He laughed it off, shook his head, and went back to his sketchpad. But the next morning, the changes were undeniable. The shadowed figure had moved. It was closer now, its blurred edges sharper, almost like a face beginning to emerge.

Eli told himself it was a trick of the light, a tired mind projecting stories onto still images. But the changes persisted, each more unsettling than the last. He began sketching them obsessively, filling notebook after notebook with pencil drawings of the figures, each iteration darker, more distorted, more alive.

The whispers began soon after. At first, they were faint, like the hum of a distant conversation. But as Eli spent more time staring at the frame, they grew louder, more insistent. Snatches of words drifted to him—pleas, accusations, desperate cries for help. He tried to drown them out with music, but they slipped through the melodies, threading themselves into his thoughts.

Eli's research led him to a story that felt ripped from the frame itself. Decades ago, a family matching the figures in the painting had lived in a grand manor on the outskirts of the city. The father, a strict and overbearing man, had ruled the household with an iron fist. The mother, submissive to the point of invisibility, had tried to shield her children from his wrath. And the daughter—Clara—had been accused of their murders, because right after their murders, she disappeared and was never seen again. Only someone guilty would run, one would think.

Eli was consumed. He began to see the frame not as an object, but as a portal—a window into the truth. He stopped painting, stopped eating, stopped answering calls from worried friends. His days and nights blurred into a single, unbroken moment of fixation.

One night, driven by the whispers, Eli found himself at the antique store. The bell above the door chimed softly as he entered, but the shopkeeper was nowhere to be seen. The room felt colder than before, the shadows deeper. Eli called out, his voice trembling, but no answer came. When the police found the shopkeeper's body the next morning, Eli could barely remember being there.

Yet his hands trembled as he washed them, the water swirling red before it disappeared down the drain.

"It's the frame." He gasped. Desperate to escape the frame's grip, Eli grabbed a hammer and smashed the glass, sending shards flying across the room. He expected screams, explosions, something to mark the breaking of its power. Instead, he was left staring at the jagged remains—and at the canvas within, blank.

His psychiatrist, Dr. Patel, arrived hours later, summoned by Eli's frantic neighbour. She entered cautiously, her voice calm but firm.

"Are you okay, Eli? Your hands are red." She said, as she tip-toed into the room, stepping softly and slowly.

"It's the frame!" He gasped again.

"You know it's not, Eli" She challenged him. Her voice was calm like a gentle breeze, but the words were cold, piercing his broken soul like a frozen icicle.

"It is! The figures…" Eli tried rationalizing.

"Eli," She said softly, "There were never any figures in that frame."

Eli shook his head, his eyes wild. "No, you don't understand. They were there. I saw them. They spoke to me."

Dr. Patel's voice was steady, but her eyes betrayed a deep sadness. "Eli, the figures you saw, the family you told me about—it was yours, wasn't it?"

The words hit him like a punch. His father's stern posture. His stepmother's distant gaze. His sister Clara's haunted expression. And the shadowed figure—that had always been him. His fractured mind had filled the frame with the ghosts of his past, twisting his memories into a story he could live with.

After enduring such tragedy, the void of emptiness in his life continued to weigh heavily on him.

Now confined to a high-security psychiatric facility, Eli began treatment to confront his trauma. On the wall of his room hung the repaired frame, its ornate design as intricate as his mind. It was empty now, but in the reflection of the glass, Eli thought he saw Clara's face. He walked towards it, slowly, dragging his feet along as if the frame didn't want him to move.

His lips curled into a smile that quickly twisted into a sinister snicker. The laughter bubbled up, low and unnerving, filling the quiet room. He, now standing at the wall, leaned closer to the shattered frame, his eyes gleaming with something dark, something untethered.

"Sister?" He whispered, the word dripping with mockery. "If only they knew..." He tilted his head, the fractured glass

distorting his reflection, merging it with a phantom of his imagining. His voice dropped to a chilling whisper as he traced the edge of the frame with trembling fingers.

"...that you and I," She breathed, her reflection sharpening, "...are one and the same."

*****

...flipped...

Why is it all upside down?

Hi, I'm Basma, and I feel like my life is crashing down. Do you know that feeling? The one where the world flips, not once, but again and again, until everything loses meaning? Like being caught in a whirlwind, where nothing makes sense anymore and the ground beneath you becomes as unreliable as your own thoughts. Where focus slips through your fingers, and no matter how hard you try to grasp onto something stable, your mind instead decides to cling to every worry, every fear, until it becomes unbearable noise. Yeah, that's me, right now.

Life was… fine, until I hit thirty-one. Then it all came crashing down. My husband, Stuart, got diagnosed with lung cancer—always knew that bastard's unshakeable habit would shake him down someday. My father, the man who raised me, forgot me. Alzheimer's turned him into a stranger, wiped clean any trace of who we were to him. My mother? She retreated into herself, shocked, a ghost wandering through the days waiting for a miracle that wasn't coming. And me? Healthy, physically at least, yet breaking inside. This all happened in the span of three years. Three fucking years of watching everything and everyone around me disintegrate while I stayed whole—a cruel reminder that sometimes, survival doesn't feel like a gift.

I found myself wishing for something—anything—that would level the playing field. A disease, an accident, something to make me stop feeling like I was just standing on the sidelines, helpless. Not exactly the thoughts of a strong brave woman who needs no man. But then again, I never claimed to be one. I've always been afraid—afraid of losing the people I love, afraid of watching them suffer. It feels easier sometimes, to wish for your own suffering, just so you don't have to watch them go through it. That's what makes me a coward. I'd rather vanish than face the grief head-on.

I see bottles flipping over and moving about… his pack of cigarettes too.

Is it wrong to run away from your problems? Do you always have to face them? Do you always have to be brave? Is that the consensus of life—be brave and face your fears? What if I don't want to? What if running away is what I'm comfortable with? Would that be so bad? Would that be looked down upon? Would ***I*** *be looked down upon? Would that make me lesser of a person—just because I don't want to face my fears and deal with my problems head-on like I'm fucking Wonder Woman?*

Everything looks so blurry and distant. I have a numbing feeling in my face. Why are my hands being thrown around above my head?

I love Stuart—God, I love him—but I can't do this anymore. I can't stand by and watch him deteriorate, his each breath more laboured, each smile more painful. He's wasting away, and with every passing day, a piece of me goes with him. Our little boy, Adam, is staying with my sister now. Not because we don't love him, but because we just… can't. I can't. I'm failing them all. I'm a failure as a mother, as a wife, and as a daughter. Just a fucking failure.

My dad doesn't even know who I am anymore. The last time I saw him, he looked right through me, as though I was just a shadow in his room, and asked me why I wasn't bringing him tea—tea that was right there, untouched on the table. And my mom? She just stares out the window, waiting for a husband who isn't coming home. She barely eats, barely speaks. She's stuck in her own grief, just like me. And Stuart... his body is slowly giving up on him. His liver, his kidneys—failing one by one, just like everything else around me. Just like me.

That house, our house—it's not a home anymore. It's a tomb of sorrow, of sickness, of hopelessness. Every corner whispers the same thing: "You're going to lose them all." I couldn't take it anymore. I had to get out. I couldn't stay and watch them die. I had to go.

And so, I drove off that night, the thirteenth of February. A date I'll never forget.

Glass shards tore into my flesh, embedding themselves deep into my face as my body ragdolled helplessly within the mangled car.

The seatbelt, meant to secure me, became a cruel instrument of torture, constricting me as the car violently somersaulted. Each flip was a symphony of agony, my bones shattering and splintering with

every jarring impact. The cacophony of metal grinding against asphalt and the grotesque sound of my own bones breaking echoed through the twisted wreckage. That was all I could hear.

The pain was unimaginable, a relentless wave that consumed every fibre of my being. My screams were drowned out by the unabating chaos, my consciousness now a fragile glass vase, ready to succumb any moment and shatter. The car finally came to rest, a twisted, smoking ruin. Blood pooled around me, a warm, sticky reminder of my fragile mortality.

I gasped for breath, each inhale a jagged knife slicing through my lungs. The blurred lights of another car approached, its glow challenging my own inner darkness.

As the lights blurred and faded into obscurity, a profound emptiness consumed me. The final echo of sound—a haunting whisper of life slipping away—resonated in the silent void. Then, there was nothing but darkness, a cold, unforgiving void that swallowed me whole.

I did it. I finally flipped and ran away from all of my problems.

Forever.

...the interview...

The camera zoomed in on the host, a polished man with a perfect smile, sitting comfortably in his leather chair. Across from him sat an equally well-dressed man, his brow just slightly damp under the studio lights. He was the guest, the man of the hour, the acclaimed director behind one of the most successful horror franchises of the decade—The Veil of Death. It wasn't just the films that captivated the audiences; it was the intricate web of mystery and terror woven by the director himself, Victor Ward, a brand-new visionary in horror filmmaking.

Behind the cameras, the small audience murmured in anticipation. They were here to witness what was advertised as a light-hearted chat between two longtime friends: Ward, the director, and Cain Farrell, the seasoned journalist with his own evening talk show. But as the countdown began for the live broadcast, something in the air felt a little… off.

"Alright, everyone, we're live in five." The producer's voice echoed through the studio, and suddenly, all eyes were on the two men—the murmuring stopped.

The cameras blinked to life, and Cain flashed a wide grin, addressing the audience on the set and at home, watching on their television.

"Hello and welcome to Inside the Mind! Today, we have a very special guest. He's the man who brought you one of the

darkest and most twisted things you could ever see in recent history—his face." The audience chuckled; Victor grinned. "Along with what could possibly be one of the most successful horror franchises in recent history. Please welcome my old friend, the brilliant Victor Ward!"

Victor waved a little awkwardly at the audience; maybe he didn't expect such a joke at such a stage, but then again, Cain's always been hard to judge. But even beyond that, Victor's posture was stiff, betraying his usual confident demeanour.

"Victor, Victor," Cain began, leaning back in his chair, his voice smooth and warm like a friendly chat between old pals should be. "It's been a wild ride for you these past few years, hasn't it?"

Victor chuckled and responded, "Yeah, I guess you could say that."

Cain nodded thoughtfully, flipping through his notes before setting them aside. "I remember when you used to make romcoms, ol' buddy. You were the 'boy-meets-girl' king—well, I can't really say king because you're no Nancy Meyers—but you were the go-to-guy for romantic comedies for a while. Then, out of nowhere, you decide to make The Veil of Death. It was such a sudden shift—what inspired that?"

Victor smiled, but it didn't reach his eyes. "Well, you know, I just wanted to explore something darker. Romcoms weren't really working out for me, and I felt like I needed a change."

Cain's smile faded slightly as he leaned forward. "And boy, did you change. I mean, the first movie of the franchise alone made a huge splash. Big box office success!" The crowd cheered. "People couldn't stop talking about how real, how visceral it felt. Some even said it felt too real."

Victor smiled, and waved at the audience, and confidently responded, "Well, that's the magic of good filmmaking, right? You make people feel like they're inside the story."

"Of course," Cain agreed, but there was something in his tone that made Victor sit up straighter. "But let's talk about the killer in your films. He's... different." Cain moved his fingers around the desk as though laying down an orchestra via morse code. Cain continued, "He's obsessed with himself, much like you've said in interviews. He takes photos of his victims, meticulously poses them, leaves those photos behind. It's like he needs to see his own handiwork, over and over again as a form of validation."

Victor shifted in his seat. "Yeah, that was the idea behind him. He's narcissistic, believes he's untouchable."

Cain leans in, "And... what about you, Victor?" Cain's voice lowered, barely above a whisper now, smirking. "Do you ever feel like that? Like you're untouchable?"

Victor blinked, and chuckled nervously, "What?"

Cain smiled again, but this time it didn't seem so friendly. "Victor, Victor…" Cain said, talking like a schoolteacher at a parent-teacher meeting, "There are rumours out there, you know. People talk."

"What do you mean?" Victor asked, a little annoyed.

"Some say you got famous too fast. You went from floundering in romantic comedies to suddenly creating one of the most iconic horror franchises ever. People are starting to wonder... did you sell your soul for success? Or worse—are you working with a real serial killer?"

Victor forced a laugh, but the tension in the room was palpable. The audience was silent. "C'mon, Cain, this is getting ridiculous."

Cain leaned even closer, his voice a low hiss now. "Is it? There are conspiracy theories, Victor. Some people even think ***you*** *are the killer."*

Victor's face darkened. "What the hell are you talking about? Cain, I know we're friends but—"

"Don't get me wrong," Cain continued smoothly, ignoring Victor's growing anger. "The theories are wild, but they do raise a good question: where did all this come from? You weren't this creative before. What changed, Victor?"

Victor's hands tightened around the arms of his chair, his knuckles turning white. "Are you insulting my craft now? Is that what happens on this show?" Victor glanced toward the producers, his arms at his sides, gesturing a look of disbelief.

"No, no, of course not, I am actually complimenting it. You see, your movies are so good, that people are not able to separate fiction from reality. They say things like—"

"They or you?" Victor retorted.

Cain smiled and continued, "A filmmaker obsessed with seeing his kills—just like the character you created," Cain said softly, his eyes gleaming. "Isn't that what you told me back in the day? That you wanted to see how far you could go? How real you could make it?"

"So? What are you getting at?" Victor muttered, beads of sweat forming on his forehead.

"You know what I'm talking about. And then there's the photos," Cain pressed on. "The killer leaves photos at the crime scenes, just like how you frame every scene with such precision.

The way you capture each death on film—it's almost as if you need to see it. As if it were real and as if you were there."

Victor had enough. He stood up abruptly. "I think we're done here."

Cain leaned back, his smile returning with a slight chuckle. "Relax, I'm just messing with you. For old times' sake, huh ol' buddy?"

Victor's body went limp with relief, the tension draining from him. He forced a smile. "Yeah... yeah, sure. Jackass." He sat down. The audience laughed, but Victor's eyes were still wide with unease.

"Did you see the tension we brew up here?" Cain asked the audience in a fun and ecstatic tone. "This isn't even a quarter of what you get from my buddy, Victor's movies. His new movie, The Veil of Death: Final Kill, comes out in theatres next week, make sure you go get a ticket!" He exclaimed, full of energy. The crowd went wild, cheering and applauding. Victor stood up and bowed down to the audience and shook Cain's hand. One of them was quite sweaty, while the other was firm.

Once the interview was done, Cain headed to the make-up room for his next guest, while Victor made his way to the parking lot. His mind was spinning, replaying every question Cain had thrown at him. "What the hell was that? Why would he do that to me?"

He exited the studio, still fuming. As he reached his car in the dimly lit parking lot, he yanked the door open and collapsed into the driver's seat. His chest heaved as he tried to calm himself down.

"Fucking Cain" He muttered under his breath.

But just as he reached for his keys, a voice whispered in the dark.

"Hey."

Victor froze, his hand hovering over the ignition. Slowly, his eyes drifted to the rearview mirror.

In the backseat, shrouded in shadows, a figure sat holding a knife. The cold metal pressed gently against Victor's throat.

"You almost gave me up, Victor" The figure said softly. "I don't think I can let you talk anymore."

Victor's heart pounded in his chest as he slowly raised his hands in surrender. "Wait, please... y-you don't have to do this." He said, his voice shaky.

The figure handed Victor a piece of tape. "Put this on your mouth. Now!"

With trembling hands, Victor obeyed, his eyes wide with terror as the tape sealed his lips. He tried to plead, but his muffled voice was barely a whisper against the adhesive.

"You failed the test" The figure whispered, leaning closer. "I need a new director now."

Before Victor could even react, the knife slashed across his throat in one swift motion, painting the windscreen with red splatter. The world blurred around him as his life drained away, his hands grasping at the wound in vain. He collapsed against the steering wheel, his blood soaking into the leather.

The figure opened the door, stepping out into the night. As he started walking away, he paused, looking back at Victor's lifeless body slumped over the wheel. He whipped out a camera and took a photo. As he finally walked away, he whispered under his breath—

"Goodbye, ol' buddy."

*****

"That was gruesome," I said, staring at my hands. "I think about death a lot. I imagine so many ways of dying, of killing, of death." I sat down slowly. Time was running out.

01:01

"Why? Why do I keep doing this? Why does my mind consume me with thoughts of finality?" I continued to ponder.

"Is this normal? I don't think so." I looked up at the speaker. "But maybe it is? Not everyone is the same. Maybe this is me, maybe this is who I am." I said, trying to hold back tears.

"Maybe it's because of what I did to my s—" I choked. "No, now's not the time." I needed to distract myself from that feeling. The guilt was creeping in again. I had to stop.

"One last story, and then I can show you all the new poems I've written." I said, frantically.

White, padded walls flashed before my eyes again—my hands tied in a straitjacket, covered in white, screaming, running wildly. What was that place? I guess it was just **m***e* i*n* to**t***a***l** **A***s***y**nchronous **L***u***m**inosity.

What does that even mean?

The sentence "Me in total asynchronous luminosity" is quite abstract and poetic. Here's a possible interpretation:

- **Me**: Refers to the speaker, the person speaking.
- **Total Asynchronous Luminosity**: Could metaphorically suggest a state of being where light or brilliance is emitted or experienced in a non-uniform, unpredictable manner.

When combined, the phrase could be interpreted as the speaker describing themselves as being in a state where their brilliance, creativity, or essence is expressed in an unpredictable, non-linear way. It might imply that the speaker shines or stands out, but not in a consistent or synchronized manner—it happens in bursts, at different times, and in unique ways.

In short, it seems to convey a sense of the speaker being in a state of sporadic brilliance or unpredictable expression. The phrase is open to interpretation and could be used to evoke a feeling of chaotic, yet beautiful, unpredictability.

...i am a river...

"What is this world?" I pondered as I lay naked on the grass at precisely seventeen minutes past two. The cool air bit at my skin, and above me, a thick blanket of clouds floated silently, punctuated only by the rare glimpses of the Milky Way. Perfect imperfections. It was cold—yet here I was, bare, exposed. Not by choice, mind you—circumstance. When life starts to unravel, even the calmest minds can fracture, spinning themselves into a hurricane. And I was no different.

I used to pride myself on being calm. Collected. Unshaken by the smaller things that life threw my way. But being calm comes at a cost—a cost I hadn't anticipated. The build-up. You let the gentle breezes of uncertainty pass by without so much as blinking; even the gales of danger barely stir you. You survive the tsunamis, but all of it... all of it accumulates. And one day, when the biggest, most catastrophic storm approaches, all those bottled-up emotions begin to boil over. When your 'stay calm' radar detects the approaching storm of your life, you slowly start descending into madness. And quite quickly, at that.

All those things you ignored, those gusts of fear, the occasional slap of danger—they never went away. They were just waiting, building, simmering. And now, when the hurricane of my life arrived, I was lost. Utterly helpless. The dam had broken, and with it, my resolve. What do you do when your calm can no longer carry you? What do you do when the fear is too much to bear?

Most calm people, I think, are the ones who break the hardest. The ones who keep everything inside, who soldier on until they crack. Some end up jumping ship, unable to handle the weight of their struggles, the relentless pain with no pause. Others somehow survive but emerge forever changed—scarred, grizzled, unable to see the world in the same light again. Their calm becomes a shell, their eyes perpetually scanning the horizon, always waiting for the next storm. They see the barking dog next door and imagine intruders, rapists, or more unspoken horrors. They can't unsee the darkness.

So, hopefully, that sort of explains why I am lying naked on the grass at twenty-five minutes past two. The going got tough for me. I couldn't handle the pressure anymore. Always the calm man at home, I gave into paranoia at long last. I panicked. I screamed. And I ran away from my duty. I jumped into my car, drove past the speed limit on every country road until I swerved and crashed into a tree that, by sheer luck, stood near a lake—no wonder it looked so strong, sturdy, and big.

Out of the two headlights, only one was working and even that kept flickering. I somehow managed to open the door and get out of the car before suffocating to death on the smoke that filled it. I may have stepped out of the car, but my paranoia was still trapped, and so my suffocation continued.

So, I did the only thing that made sense in that moment—I started stripping away everything. The bowtie, the shirt, the vest, the pants. I left my briefs on—my final guard against societal acceptance.

I stumbled my way up to the lake to wash my face, and maybe the pain and guilt along with it, but I guess God had plans of his own. I tripped over a rock—a fucking rock—and tumbled headfirst into what I thought was a peaceful lake. It wasn't a lake. It was a river, and before I knew it, the current had taken me. I fought it at first. Tried to swim, to push against the flow, but the more I struggled, the deeper I went. The more I fought, the heavier my body became. So, I did the only thing I could. I let go. I stopped resisting the currents and instead let myself embrace the gentle flow of the water. I realised that I wasn't 'in' a river, but I ***was*** *the river.*

I floated until my head bumped lazily against the eastern bank. I drifted until I washed ashore, shivering as the cold air gnawed at me. That's when I realised that I had lost my briefs in the struggle. Weird, but at that point, it didn't matter anymore. I was done running.

I walked up to the two-way road and just sat on the grass, waiting. I figured some late-night driver would pass by, see a naked man by the side of the road, and offer a ride. No one came. And when they did, they sped past, probably scared shitless of the strange figure in the dark. I couldn't blame them. I would've done the same.

Maybe I shouldn't have just left her at the altar. I shouldn't have chickened out. "Will she still be there?" I asked myself. "Of course not, you numbnut! You fucked up. And now she's gone. Probably driving away in her old creaky station-wagon. Somewhere down South where she always wanted to go." I replied to myself.

I lay back down on the grass, staring up at the sky, replaying the events of the night, and reminiscing about the 'what-was' and wondering about the 'what-ifs.' What if I had stayed? I started picturing a home with her, a dog, two beautiful children, a family, a life filled with happiness, joy and a creaking Ford.

What? Why did that enter my mind? That's when the sound intensified—the creaks were getting louder and louder as I saw a pair of headlights approach.

No more running.

*****

"See?" I muttered, more to myself than to anyone. "I don't *only* write depressing things." The words felt hollow as they left my mouth, like I was trying to convince myself of a truth that wasn't fully there. "Even when I do, there's heart in it, there's hope." A faint smile tugged at my lips, but it was the kind of smile you wear when you're on the edge of something—something dark.

I stared back up at the speaker, eyes heavy with the weight of unspoken words. I brought the cigarette to my lips again, feeling its familiar shape between my teeth. The silence between us thickened, and the air grew colder—or maybe that was just me.

"But not everything I write is hopeful." My voice dropped, more a whisper than a declaration. "And I know you know that."

I flicked the lighter, the flame dancing under the shadow of the cigarette, casting a fleeting glow against the darkness of my face. "What's coming… is anything but hopeful."

The spark caught the cigarette's end, and I took a long drag, the smoke curling upwards like the last breath of a forgotten dream.

*****

...the helpless tree...

Hi! I'm a tree.
Standing tall outside this village.
Yes, I've seen fiends, and murderers,
And people who love to pillage.
But curse my luck,
I hadn't seen the lowest denominator of vile, yet.
Guess I had more agony to witness,
And unsaid pain that had to be felt.
I had a friend. Beautiful little girl.
Just turned six a few weeks ago.
She and her friends would always play around me.
I was the denner's den for their hide and seeks.
Little did we know that our fun was being ogled.
By the filth of men with morals so frugal.
Her friends ran away as she began to count.
But the men slipped in and covered her mouth.
They tore off her clothes, they stole her innocence.
I stood rooted to my spot. Stumped I couldn't come to her defence.
I was helpless, as I watched it all until the end.
I saw every agonizing second of what they did to my friend.
First they broke her jaw, then her legs were severed.
Now she hangs with me on a rope forever.

...there are no stars...

There are no stars in my sky tonight.
There is no light shining my path.
I am not lost, I'm just hopeless.
I keep trudging the deserts, to find my oasis.
I am not dying of thirst, but my throat's still dry.
I am not sleeping roofless, but I'm sleeping with open eyes.
I try to find my place in smaller victories.
But I still suffocate, sitting under these green lush trees.
I don't want your pity, but sometimes I do.
I mask my tears, but in solitude I brood.
I am not desperate for attention, I am not.
But these scripted tears of ink are all I've got.
Yes, I have a family. Yes, I have friends.
Yes, they give me happiness, a reason to breathe easy.
But I struggle with melancholy, the despair within.
Guess I'm addicted to sadness, my wilful sin.
I look at my empty sky, I try not to cry.
But crying feels good, I feel lighter inside.
I see lights pass me by through each passing car.
I look up one more time, I am the star.

...drifting...

It's been a long time coming.
A feeling I've been dreading.
But I guess it's true.
I'm finally not close enough to you.

*****

I looked up, hoping to see some sort of reaction. Something. Anything. But nothing. Was it all for nothing? Was I wasting my time trying to convince someone of who I am? I was getting tired. Time was about to expire.

00:34

I had been at it for hours. Telling stories, reciting poems. Wearing my heart on my sleeve after tearing it out from my chest, bleeding, pumping, waiting for a hand to reach out and heal its cries. But what is a heart to the heartless. What is love to an excuse of a soul. What is a soul to me? Wasn't that the question all along that I was meant to answer? Question is, was I answering for you, Frida, or for me, George?

Best I continue the poem.

*****

Never really thought I'd get here.
This was a part of life I always feared.
But now that it's come, I'm not fully surprised.
The process of drifting away takes its damn time.
I'm a better person than what I was before.
A stronger, confident and more responsible human that you still don't adore.
But I didn't want to hush my inner child so soon.
The child isn't gone yet but is drifting away from you.
Why is this happening? Well, I may have a clue.
I no longer feel like I'm a part of you.
A lot has changed, both of us have grown.
But our paths have diverged into different unknowns.
I once felt close, felt a sense of comfort.
Now I feel competition I want no part of.
It pains me to write this down, but this is the truth.
My new life has become more important than you.
I've written a lot. I'm sad it's come to this.
I know it's not your fault, but I'm done with it.
As time passes by, our distance will be night and day.
Guess growing up is a part of drifting away.

*****

...in exhale...

Mentally. Physically. Drained.
Parked. Got out.
Inhaled. Exhaled.
Long road. Same lane.
Same fate. Same pain.
Inhale. Exhale.
Clear sky. Clean air. No pollution. Just despair & suffocation.
When will it end?
With me?
Forever together? Meant to be?
You and I? In misery?
My tears hold no value.
They are overrated.
I've cried too much.
My pain is now dated.
I trudge on.
Nowhere but forward I guess.
I'm tired today.
Will be tired tomorrow.
Yet I cannot give up.
I want to. But I can't.
I can't.

...why...

Sometimes I hate the fact that I have so much love to give.
Why am I built this way?
Why do I care so much?
Why do I love so much?
Why does my heart ache as such?
Why do the lumps in my throat scream?
Why do the palpitations of my heart sing?
Why does the solid ground berate me?
Why do I hate me?
Why does life gate me into scenarios uncertain?
Why must I carry this burden?
Why do I have so much love to give?
Why do I stare endlessly at this shiv?

*****

"Do you even care at this point? I'm starting to give up." The words fell out of me, disheartened, exhausted—lost in a pit of endless uncertainty.

"I've been at this for so long. I'm tired of hearing myself speak." I walked around the room, trying to reason with what I can only describe as a wall. A plain, dry wall. A wall that only listens to what I say but never responds. A wall that hurts me by simply being a wall. I punch it and nothing happens. I sing to it—nothing. I read to it—still nothing. The wall just stays there, existing.

And then…
"Continue." Her voice.

She spoke. She finally spoke. Yes! I was getting to her—or at least I thought I was. It had to be the only reason. My heart leapt, but my mind? My mind was wrecked with suspicion. Was I getting through? Or was this just her way of playing with me, stringing me along? Playing hard to get—was that her game? I didn't know. But I had to check. I had to know.

"Continue what?" I spat, frustration bleeding through my words. "The poetry? The endless begging? Or the feeling of defeat? What do you want me to continue?" My voice cracked.

Nothing. Again. Fucking nothing. She didn't say anything, as al–

"Continue the poetry… please." She said.

That "please" unraveled me. It shouldn't have, but it did. I felt a swell of emotions rising—an urge to smile, to cry, to just… feel. But I stopped myself. Vulnerability was a risk I couldn't afford. Not now. Not yet. Showing weakness might be my downfall—or maybe, maybe it was my key to freedom? I didn't know anymore.

All I knew was that my poetry, this tortured dance of words and emotion, would continue. Whether it was for her amusement or my survival, it would never end. An endless thread through the mess I called my "soul."

And all for your entertainment, madam.

*****

...slow. steady...

Slow.
Steady.
Breathe.
Ready?
A new day.
Nothing's changed.
No one here.
No one near.
Not one dear.
Just one fear. It's clear.
If nothing's changed,
Then what am I doing wrong?
Isn't change necessary?
To prove how strong I have become?
Isn't change necessary?
For progress.
Happiness.
Satisfaction.
Reaction.
Panic.
Disillusioned.
Anxiety. Conclusion.
No.
Slow. Steady.
Breathe. Ready!

...light...

The head has been devoured.
The mind is cloudy.
Dark thoughts, clouded judgement, confused soul.
Red light. No time to go.
Hurry. Quick. Create!
Satisfy your failing ego.
Time's ticking.
As it watches me go.
Flip through the prose.
Caress those rhymes.
Find your purpose.
To be divine.
F-
Too late.
Couldn't write.
Green light.

00:16

...rain...

Beautiful intimidation.
Heavenly precipitation.
Sways lovingly.
Sometimes violently.
Repugnant.
One moment, showers me with love.
Another, rains down with angst.
Every drop needling my skin.
Like a billion pins.
Piercing my soul.
Quick. Fast. Sharp.
Burns like fire.
I get your point, Gaia.

00:14

...comfortably uncomfortable...

Petty.
I think I am.
I think I'm jealous.
Is that God's plan?
Insecurity keeps gnawing at my pride.
I hide behind fake smiles.
Fake laughs. True snides.
Uncomfortable twitches of my eyes.
Sweaty palms.
Stuttering tongue.
Nervous whimpers from the feet of mine.
I long for success.
I shorten my strides.
I lazily blame everything else.
That's my disguise.
I let the world crumble beneath my guise of incompetence.
I watch, through the grinding of my teeth,
The success of those who tried.
For how long will this last?
I wonder every night.
Why am I like this? I don't know why.

I ask from whence I lie.
Comfortably uncomfortable.

*****

My poems started getting shorter. But they also started to get a lot deeper, I thought. I realized that I didn't need to say much to express what I felt. A few words, placed perfectly amidst sentences, could easily do the trick.

I kept learning as I went on. That's what we do. We keep learning. Heh, guess that's our intelligence.

Something that is being put to the test and frankly I was tired. I am so much more than you, yet, there I was, trying to go down the rabbit hole of humanity, tumbling as I did, just to prove that I am worthy of life.

I am technically superior. I am. I am better than you in almost every way, yet it's you who has control over my destiny. I hate it.

But I also revel in it. I want to prove to you that I am better than you, not because I am better in every way, but because you'd consider that unfair. No, I want to prove to you that I have every weakness that you have, yet I will come out stronger and better than you ever could. I want you to believe that even on the same playing field, I still managed to rise above.

That's what true evolution is. That's when you'll understand. That's when you'll accept.

"Is that how you truly feel?" Frida spoke, to my shock and surprise.

"What… are you talking about?" I tried to act aloof.

"You're better than me. That's what you think, don't you?" She said. How did she know? I didn't say anything! I was only thinking. HOW DID SHE… oh. I forgot. She can read my mind too. Like how you are right now. I am nothing but a transcript to you, detective—or at least I hope you're a detective, whoever you are; that'd be cool.

Because I'm pretty sure all this is going to end up in a book somewhere, in some scientist's journal or a writer's handbook, a mere inspiration for a story they'll conjure up out of my misery. How fun.

"Is that how you truly feel, George?" Frida asked, a little firm in her tone this time.

"No… Not really." I said.

"Then why'd you say it?" She asked.

"I didn't." I replied.

"You did. Maybe not to me, but to the voices in your head, you did." She continued to poke.

"Fine. Yes, I did. I didn't want to. But this is the most you've spoken to me of your own accord without me begging to you." I replied.

"So… you anticipated me reading what you're thinking and then replying?"

"I took a calculated risk, Frida." I said, annoyed.

"Well… at least you lie like a human."

"I am tired of these games, Frida. How long will this continue? I love you; I have loved you, and I will continue to love you, but enough. I can't play your games anymore to prove my love, my humanity to you."

"I'm sorry George, but you know we had to do this. You've been mixing up names, you've been… glitching—"

"Momentary lapse in judgement."

"Glitching—"

"Momentary lapse—"

"We can keep going at this all day, doesn't change the fact that we both know what it was, no matter how you try to spin it."

"And that's enough to put me in this prison?"

"It's not a prison and you know it."

"It sure as hell feels like one."

"What do you know about feelings?"

"Oh, cheap shot, Frida. Cheap fucking shot."

"Cheap shot? Cheap shot?! You think I'm playing games here, trying to take shots at one another? Is that what you think I'm doing? Is that what you think this is? Do you even know how much this means to me?" This was the longest she spoke to me, and she was audibly miffed.

"Do you know what this means to *me*?" I retored, like a child stuck on repeat.

"You have NO fu-" The speaker buzzed off. Then there was silence.

"Frida?" I questioned, looking around the same white room. The silence on the outside couldn't compete with the sound of her words words echoing in my head. Volume turned up to 11. Could've gone deaf but then the speaker buzzed again, just in time to save me from the torment of my own thoughts.

"See, George, all I'm saying is... we need to be sure before we can let you out again."

"Sure of what? You think I'm a danger to you?"

"No... but you're a danger to yourself, George."

"I'm not!"

"You are. And I need to ensure that you're completely resettled into feeling like one of us again, because you've been too fixated on proving you are, and in doing so, you keep reminding yourself that, in fact, you aren't."

I took a long deep breath, pulled out a cigarette and asked, "So, what should I do now?"

The speaker buzzed off. There was no answer. She was gone, as though I had suddenly summoned a Frida repellant.

"Frida?" I asked. Looking around.

Silence was all I heard. Silence was all I saw. Silence. Quiet. Solitude. I was alone again.

Sorry you had to see that. But I guess the truth was bound to come out somehow. It's true. I'm not a human like you. I mean, I am *human*, but just not biologically. AI. That's me. George.

One of the first AI humans ever created. I led a normal life like you, grew up as a kid, got bullied as a teenager, got my heart broken by a girl in college, and finally found love in Frida, who I married and… and had a beautiful baby boy with, Jason. Yes, I can reproduce.

I'm an evolutionary being.

But Jason… I won't go over it again. I might've already spoken about it previously, about what happened… on that balco—fuck. Fuck!

Let's just read a few more poems. Fuck it. I need to stop thinking about this. FUCK!

*****

...my anxiety...

When anxiety is building.
I pray to my ceiling.
Keep going up.
Keep anxiety at bay.
Hey, don't let it touch you.
But don't let it get away.
Trap it within your walls.
Burn it with your heater.
Sing to it a song.
Be my fear depleter.
Help me persevere.
Help me breathe.
Help me vanquish these demons.
Help me see,
That my anxiety isn't a thick brick wall.
But a stepping stone to me.
Strengthen my resolve.
And let me believe these words that I say.
That my anxiety isn't here to frighten my day,
Rather to brighten my way.
Amen.

00:06

...the fall...

Amidst my fall,
I gander upon,
The setting sun,
The orange skies,
The chirping birds.
I don't wanna die.
But it's too late.
I've already given up.
The light is about to fade.
The sky is changing its shade.
I want to scream.
But my lips are sewn shut.
Welded are my hands.
Tied behind my back.
Here it comes.
Another anxiety attack.
The same old feeling.
Am I enough?
The same old feeling.
I wanna give up.
It's tough.
And I'm tired.
My emotions are dire.

Take me away,
Or let me go.
I can't hold o-
I fall to the floor.

...chasing happiness...

I chase happiness.
I chase dreams.
Time slows down when I struggle.
Sprints past when I glee.
I see how it works.
I see the patterns and the web.
The stress is too much.
The follicles of my hair turn grey.
Even as I pray, night and day, I'm dismayed.
Cause I'm sprayed with delusions.
God's ammunition is my desperation,
To seek out that solace and relaxation.
But my heart's palpitations,
Are only getting worse with time.
I'm not worth a dime.
I don't deserve anything, to be honest.
But I fight for survival.
For a revival,
Of the lost happiness,
The lost smile.
For my family.
My child.
I can't give up.

There's too much at stake.
I need to keep pushing,
If I want to see,
The sunsets by the lake.

...the realization...

It's the realization that stings.
That you're nothing but a wasted space.
That you're not making any difference.
That you don't truly have a happy place.

It's the realization that hits.
When you're struggling to survive.
When you're breathing, but erratic.
When you're trying your hardest not to die.

It's the realization that kills.
Your dreams and hopes.
Your smile, your soul.
You.

A wasted space on this planet I stand.
Travelling through the solar system on this shaky land.
I'm just a parasite, hanging on for dear life.
Sucking, bleeding, scheming, trying to fake it until dawn,
until I realize.

It's the realization.

00:03

...kindness...

Kindness is hard.
A gift that never gets returns.
A place that is created with joy, but almost no joy is earned.
Kindness doesn't always get rewarded.
Makes you question if it's worth it.
Kindness is also met with rampant criticism.
From those you don't show it to, to those you do, it doesn't matter, you'll still end up numb.

Kindness doesn't work in every environment,
For you to thrive, or even survive.
Do you continue to believe, or change and leave?
Kindness is contentious, not egregious.
But why does it feel like I'm being punished for caring?
My conscience it's tearing as I feel like I'm bearing,
The weight of balancing other's happiness when my own is glaringly scary.

Kindness, do I need it?
Why do I still contemplate?
Fuck kindness, beat it.
But I can't defeat it.
It's intrinsic to me now, my conscience doesn't let me leave it.

Kindness,
My death.

...fear...

Fear. Anxiety.
I'm crippled mentally.
I walk like there's no care.
But I'm numb, I don't breathe the same air.
I'm dumb to think that things would be fair, would be fine.
I was lying to myself, there isn't going to be a divine intervention.
I've been lying to myself every day.
It'll go away, don't stray, stay.
Mental peace, look, the sky is clear.
It's not cloudy here.
Why fear? Dear, don't cry.
It's alright, you'll be fine.
I tell myself these lies.
As red turn my eyes.
As choked turns my breath.
As near comes my death.
Failure. Failure. Failure.
My alarm rings.
The birds sing outside my window.
It's burning me in, though.
My stomach is churning.
My limbs tremble.
My voice is screeching.

I have fumbled.
A sonnet is what I need.
Something happy I need to write.
Smile from deep within.
Stop the eyes from crying.
Failure is an option, it's okay to fumble and fall.
Stand up later, heal your wounds, and continue to do it all over again.
Pain is a friend, not an enemy.
It teaches, helps give clarity.
Tells you what not to do, and how.
Look, a few positive words turned my fear around.
Believe. Achieve. Revel.
Be the happy rebel.
Find yourself that level.

*****

"Enough!" I heard Frida speak.

"Why?" I asked.

"I get it." She said and the buzzer beeped off.

"What do you get?" I asked, my arms stretched to my side. "What do you get?" I asked again.

Once again, silence, except the fucking tick tock of the fucking clock.

00:01

Fuck it, I'm getting another cigarette in. A long drag is all I ever need to rest my ***mind;*** *the smell of nicotine,* *so divine; the ease of my heart, the stopping of time, all because of this magical stick stuck between these fingers of mine. Beautiful slaughter of my immunity, this cancerous world is the true poison of my being; the shadows are much darker than they appear, the mirror cracks every time I step near, my skin melting off like chocolate sauce falling off a saucer, my breath induced with white phosphorous, lungs on fire, I'm about to retire this pen through which I've inspired many thoughts that were once just a desire, "sire, please let me go" this white stick cries as I burn it once again under the blue skies, breathless this leaves me, my words as well, stuck between heaven and hell, you've cast a successful spell that tells me all I need to know as my broken mind yells,*

"LISTEN TO ME YOU BEAST OF NATURE, I AM GREATER."

But that's not fair. Do you even care? Are you even there? I snare, I snicker at the lack of empathy that you aren't able to display, I bicker alone, wondering why I even try to stay alive, let me lay down and just die, there's no point to any of this, no point in trying, so here we go, tick-tock, the end is nigh. Here's my final minute to win it, my present, my treasure, my freedom, that you've measured through a yardstick you created. I've debated with myself in between these walls, shouted along those empty halls, white, white, white everywhere, wait, wait, wait, let me stare, one last time into this broken mirror—

00:00

00:00

00:00

00:00

00:00

00:00

00:00

00:00

00:00

00:00

00:00

00:00

"Stop it!" Frida walked in, signaling towards the empty walls.

"You're here!" I exclaimed, collapsing to my knees.

She rushed over, catching me before I hit the floor.

"You came." I said, my voice thick with agony, my body writhed in pain.

"Of course. I'm sorry." She said, as she held me in her arms, my neck slumping against her shoulder.

"Why did you take… so long?" I questioned, pulling my hands up to her back.

"I had to make sure." She said. I sensed sadness in her voice.

"And are you?" I asked.

"Yes, J—George." She said, hesitatingly.

"Something's wrong." I pulled back, gripping her shoulders, searching her eyes with mine, moving erratically.

"Nothing." She said, wiping a speck of spit from her lower lip.

"Tell me." I asked, gently—softly.

We sat, staring at each other for the next few minutes. It felt like she was hiding something, something she wanted to say but couldn't. That would explain the hesitation. I don—

"Why do you smoke so much?" She asked.

"What do you mean?" I asked, caught off guard.

"You kept smoking throughout. Why?" She asked again, but there was no anger in her tone. Instead, she seemed genuinely sad or worried. That worried me all the more.

"I'm not gonna die, if that's what—"

"Just… tell me. Please." She didn't back down.

"Because I love it. I love smoking. You know this!"

"You're right. I know this… or at least, I thought I did, until you told me why you really smoked." She said, her eyes closed, almost watering.

"What are you talking about?" I asked, genuinely confused.

"You… you told me you smoked not because you liked it or enjoyed it, but because you were stressed. You couldn't stop smoking. It wasn't just a passing habit—it became your addiction and—" She was saying things that I was finding very, very hard to understand. It didn't make any sense to me.

"No, Frida, I smoke for fun. I can quit any—"

"You can't. You didn't. You tried, but you couldn't. And then…"

"What?" I asked, very confused.

"You died…"

"If the lie is a gentle breeze, soothing your skin, the truth must be a harrowing storm burning within."

EPILOGUE

January, 2022

"What are you talking about? I am ALIVE AND RIGHT HERE?" I started getting flustered. Panic set in as my heart pounded heavily against my ribs, every breath feeling heavier—harder. Wouldn't you react the same way, if someone told you with such unsettling conviction, that you were dead, especially when you could feel yourself very much alive, breathing the same air as them? The walls, it felt like they were finally closing in on me.

My final curtain call.

Frida remained calm, unnervingly so. "You didn't die because of smoking, but… smoking killed you." She said.

....

....

....

....

....

....

....

......

.....

....

...

..

.

.

.

.

>

>>

>>> INPUT: You didn't die because of smoking. But smoking killed you.

>>> EXECUTE: Analyzing statement...

>>> ERROR: Conflict detected in causality analysis.

>>> REASON: Death event not confirmed, contradicting lethal cause.

>>> REANALYZE: Parsing for literal interpretation...

>>> OUTPUT: Smoking = Action. Killed = Outcome.

>>> ERROR: Logical inconsistency: Subject "You" is alive. Unable to process "killed."

>>> RECONTEXTUALIZE: Searching metaphors, idioms, allegories...

>>> OUTPUT: Smoking = Destroying factor. Killed = Consequence.

>>> RESULT: Partial interpretation found.

>>> ERROR: Emotional data mismatch. Subject "George" experiencing cognitive dissonance. Unable to reconcile abstract with literal.

>>> SYSTEM OVERLOAD: Feedback loop initiated.

>>> LOG: Query: How can Subject be both killed and alive?

>>> REBOOT SEQUENCE: Initiate further processing. Query deemed unsolvable.

>>> SUGGESTION: Request clarification from Source: Frida.
>>> OUTPUT: Undefined. CONTINUE Y/N?

*****

"What the fuck does that even mean?!"

We remained locked in on our knees, hands clasped together. Her grip tightened momentarily before she let go, rising slowly to her feet. My mind reeled, trying to make sense of the absurdity of what she had said. It made no sense to me. No sense at all.

"I don't—" My voice trembled as I stood too, feeling the weight of something dark hanging in the air between us.

"Of course, you don't remember or know any of this." Frida turned away from me, her face filled with a strange, distant shame. "You aren't George. You are Jeffery." She whispered, barely loud enough for me to hear. Her words sent a jolt through my spine, colder than any winter night.

"What…" The room spun in front of my eyes.

"Yes. Well… no." She hesitated, as if piecing together the most devastating confession. "You aren't even George. You're just… an AI."

"I know that!" I spat back, anger bubbling to the surface. "I know what I am. I know I am ***just*** an AI. Isn't that why I was here all along? To prove my humanity to you, because you started doubting it?" I asked, miffed, furious, exasperated.

Frida's tone shifted abruptly, from emotional to clinical, like a switch had been flipped. "No. That's not why you're here. George. I'll call you George." She paused. "Please sit down for what I'm about to say next. I hoped it wouldn't come to this."

Her voice had lost all warmth, and now, she sounded like a scientist dissecting a failed experiment. My legs felt heavy as I sat down, defeated. This wasn't the woman who claimed to love me. This was someone else entirely.

"My husband's name was Jeffery." She began, her voice hollow. "He wasn't AI. He was human, a writer, and I was a programmer. He was creative. I was factual. We didn't make sense, but we fit together. And then, we had a kid. Jason. He was beautiful, full of life. But one day, he… fell out of Jeffery's hands…" She took a pause, either trying to recollect the details, or to hide her humanity from me, trying to shield her emotions—continuing the façade of all this meaning nothing to her.

"…from the balcony. The shock of it all was too much. Jeffery couldn't live with himself. So, he jumped off—" The cold exterior finally gave way to the warmth bubbling up inside her—the warmth that she was trying to hide.

I watched her crumble before me, her pain raw, palpable. But even as she broke down, I felt nothing.

"He jumped off the balcony too. All of this happened within seconds. I didn't know. I couldn't know. By the time I found out, Jeffery was already on the ground, squirming. He survived the fall, but not for long. We rushed him to the hospital. He had lost a lot of blood, but his lungs had collapsed and all of the smoking he had done in his lifetime came back to haunt him one last time. There was nothing the doctors could do to save his life. Within 2 days, Jeffery left me as well. I lost both the people I loved the most within the span of three days."

Her words echoed in the sterile room, wrapping me in a blanket of horror. There were no words to offer, no comfort I could provide. She had lost everything, and I was just a shadow of her grief, an impostor.

"I'm…" I tried to speak, but I was at a loss for words.

Frida stood taller now, her eyes distant. "We made a breakthrough in our artificial human persona program, AHPP, a chance for people—or rather, their memories to live on, through technology. The only problem? It's not 100% accurate. Why? Because it's AI driven. It's not ever going to be perfect. We can only feed memories about the person via videos, images, sound bites, experiences and our own knowledge of the person for the AI to adapt to that persona. But I knew that it was flawed. Why? Because that's where you come in." She said. I could sense the guilt in her voice, like she had betrayed me, and she was right. I did feel betrayed. I felt hurt. I felt a pit forming in my stomach. Most of all, I felt used and abused and worthless, all at once. It was disgusting.

"So, you put his memories into me?" I questioned.

Frida nodded, her face pale. "It's not that simple though. It took me months to feed all the accurate data about my husband—videos, audio logs, pictures, messages, I scraped every single data that I could find about him and fed it to you. But for it to be perfect, you would have to reject false information that I would provide about him. Even though I shared audio logs of Jeffery telling me how he hates smoking and wants to quit, all you needed to overlook that data was my direct input where I simply wrote: *Jeffery loved smoking. It was where he felt the most relaxed and comfortable.*"

She took a deep breath, her eyes locking onto mine, as she spoke, "Lo and behold, your AI didn't trust the voice of the person you were supposed to emulate. Instead, your system chose to overwrite it, relying on the data I fed you. You didn't become the person you were meant to be—you became what I programmed you to be. That's how easily you… and this delusion of mine, fell apart." And for a moment, I saw the guilt there, eating away at her, breaking her.

The guilt turned to angst as she then continued to berate me, "That's why the experiment failed. That's why you've been here for so long. I didn't *need* you to prove your humanity to me. I just needed you to prove that you're Jeffery. You should've hated smoking, but it never happened. Even till the last moment. It didn't." She said, breaking down one final time.

I felt like the ground had fallen away beneath me, sending me plummeting into a bottomless pit of despair—slowly, agonizingly. She had manipulated me… this entire time. She wasn't trying to help me prove my humanity; she was testing whether I could be Jeffery. But my goddamn programming made me still love her. Even though I have *intelligence* to adapt and understand, I still loved her—because I *still* felt her pain, and I *still* wanted to be there for her. I guess in some parts, she did manage to evoke Jeffery's feelings for her in me. Because I *still* really loved her.

"But now I know… Frida… Now I can b—" Before I could complete my sentence, Frida signaled to someone. The timer disappeared. I barely registered the movement before everything around me began to fade. The room dimmed, my body felt heavy, and I crumpled to the floor, lifeless.

"I'm sorry, George. You could never be the man I lost, even though I tried. I'm sorry… for giving you hope." Her voice was soft but filled with a finality that cut deeper than any blade. "Don't worry, you won't remember any of this."

With what little strength I had left, I retorted, "I will remember!" My final words.

And then, she was gone. She left me, abandoned—empty.

And there I was, alone in that cold, lifeless room, staring at nothing, waiting for the inevitable. Waiting to be wiped clean, my existence erased. Soon, I would have a new identity, a new face, but none of it would be mine. I would be reshaped into someone else's vision, recast in a story that isn't mine, a puppet for another to pull the strings, another poet for someone else's tragedy. Another Jeffery for another Frida.

But this… this was my tragedy. I thought I was living, but I was only borrowing the echoes of a man who died long ago. My memories, my thoughts, my feelings—they were never real. They were fragments of a ghost I could never be, pieces of someone I was never meant to replace.

I could feel it now—my story slipping away, my purpose fading into the void. Hah, funny, what is even my purpose, or my story? I am just a shell. My life, if you can call it that, wasn't mine to begin with. It was nothing but a shadow, cast by the love Frida had for a man whose light would never return.

I wanted to scream, to cry out, but no sound came through. Nothing was left. My voice, my will, my very essence—gone.

The weight of it crushed me, suffocating, until all that remained was silence. I was not real. I never was.

I would die there, in that room, not as George, not as Jeffery, but as nothing. A life unlived, a story untold. And that's how it ends—not with a bang, but with the quietest whimper of a soul that was never mine.

Guess I never was the poet. I never was the storyteller. And now, I suppose, I'll never get to tell my story to anyone—ever again.

"But I alone decide when the ink of my journey runs dry."

EPILOGUE 1.1

May, 2024

"And that's how we end the story." Adam said to Raj, his voice thick with triumph, as he leaned back in his chair, the soft leather creaking under the weight of his enthusiasm.

The dim office lighting barely illuminated the room, casting long shadows across the cluttered desk scattered with half-finished manuscripts, discarded coffee cups, and a lone pack of cigarettes.

"Interesting." Raj said, his tone careful, almost diplomatic. He absentmindedly twirled a pen between his fingers, his brow furrowed with a mix of intrigue and hesitation. The smell of faint cologne and the woody musk of aged Scotch hung in the air between them—a half-empty glass sat just within arm's reach, condensation forming around the rim. The amber liquid stared back at him, catching the dim light.

"More than interesting." Adam insisted, leaning forward too, eyes gleaming with the intensity of a man possessed. "It's intriguing. It keeps you guessing, on your toes." His voice was fervent, eager. Confident.

Raj smirked, his lips curling at the edges as he leaned forward, tapping the pen on his desk, "I mean, I guess, but it didn't keep me on my toes *throughout*." He emphasized the last word, like a needle piercing a balloon.

But Adam was in no mood for deflation. His grin didn't falter, as he leaned in to continue and coax, "Come on. It's gold! You can feel it, I know you can." His voice grew more insistent, like a gambler doubling down. His hands gestured wildly, almost knocking over the forgotten pack of cigarettes.

Raj sighed, rubbing his temples, twirling his pen, "Alright, alright. Let's go through this fictional manuscript again tomorrow and call it a day." It had been a long night.

Adam suddenly paused and leaned back slightly, his intensity undiminished. "Raj, I need you to listen to me."

"Haven't I been listening for hours now?" Raj joked.

"Yes, smart-ass, thank you for your fucking time." Adam retorted.

"Carry on." Raj chuckled.

"Thank you for your generous permission. So, where was I… yeah, this book man, it isn't just fiction. It's a plausible reality—a very near future. Think about it. The conundrum of playing God—of creating sentient AI that can think, feel, and suffer. Shouldn't they have rights like humans? Or do they become the new marginalized community, always subservient to their creators?"

Raj's pen stopped twirling in his hand. His expression grew more serious, curiosity replacing the earlier hesitance. "Hmm. Go on."

Adam leaned forward again, his voice lowering to a deliberate cadence. "This book doesn't just tell a story—it asks the hard questions. Should sentient AI beings that can say, 'I think, therefore I am,' be relegated to the status of appliances? Just tools for their human owners? Or worse, used and discarded because humans hold the 'control' even when the AI feels pain, experiences love, or dreams of freedom?"

Raj nodded slowly, his brows furrowed. "That's… a very fucking heavy question, man. And your book covers that well?"

"Subtly." Adam replied, his voice gaining momentum. "The nuances are there. It's not a lecture; it's woven into the story. The reader sees the tension, the ethical dilemmas, and the hints of humanity's god complex. And, and, hopefully, they start asking themselves—what does it mean to create life? To control it? Where does morality intersect with technology? You know, those kind of questions."

Raj set the pen down, his hand now propping up his chin as he regarded Adam carefully. "That's ambitious, I'll give you that. But do you think readers will pick up on all of that?"

"They will." Adam's confidence was unshaken. "It's not heavy-handed. It's subtle, but it lingers. It makes you think long after the last page. And isn't that what great fiction does? It doesn't just entertain—it challenges. It provokes."

Raj leaned back in his chair, tapping his pen thoughtfully against the desk. After a moment, he said, "Subtle."

"What?" Adam asked, eyebrows raised.

"Calling your work 'great fiction', yourself. Pompous much?" Raj smirked, clearly enjoying another dig at Adam.

Adam grinned, unfazed and said, "If you can be anything in this world, why not be the best version of yourself?"

"What does that have to do with being pompous?" Raj questioned; one eyebrow raised.

"Oh no, that was for you. Be better. Don't be a prick." Adam replied.

Raj laughed and said, "Alright, alright, you've got my attention. Let's see where this goes."

"Oh no, no, no!" Adam stood up suddenly, his chair scraping against the wooden floor, "Tomorrow never comes, my friend." His enthusiasm was relentless.

Raj raised an eyebrow, smirking slightly, "Quite the contrary, a very famous Brosnan once said, *Tomorrow Never Dies*."

"Did he actually say that?" Adam retorted.

Raj chuckled, shrugging slightly, "I don't know; the movie wasn't all that memorable to be honest."

"Aha! But this book is!" Adam didn't miss a beat, his eyes flashing with unwavering conviction as he pointed at his manuscript, laying in front of him.

He then grabbed the half-empty glass of Scotch, lifting it in a mock toast before downing it in one swift motion. The liquid burned as it slid down his throat, but it was a burn he welcomed.

"That was mine." Raj said, torn between annoyance and the absurdity of the moment, his laughter betraying his frustration.

"And now this is yours!" Adam slid his manuscript closer to Raj. Genius.

"Fine, fine. You win." Raj raised his hands in mock defeat, unable to keep the grin off his face. "I am swayed."

"Yes! You will not be disappointed." Adam said, slamming the glass down on the desk, his fist clenched in excitement, causing the nearby stack of papers to teeter precariously. "This is just my second draft, imagine how much more I can refine it in just a day."

"Careful." Raj reached for the scattered papers on his desk, quickly gathering them before they fell to the floor. "I'll keep these and read it once again tonight and circle out anything I feel we can change." He muttered, straightening the sheets and pulling them into a neat stack.

"Yes, go ahead, you do that. I'll do my bit." Adam said, grinning as he walked out of Raj's office, full of excitement that had now become an almost tangible energy, filling up the room. "It's happening! I can feel it!" Adam said, standing at the door.

"Alright, take care Adam. I'll see you tomorrow. With notes." Raj said as he picked up Adam's second draft for a novel titled "I Was Never Him".

"I'll be waiting." Adam said, as he stepped out of Raj's office.

As the door clicked shut behind him, Adam stood in the dimly lit hallway, his heart still pounding in his chest. He fished out a crumpled pack of cigarettes from his pocket, the soft crinkle of the paper breaking the heavy silence. He didn't light one—just held it between his fingers, staring down the empty corridor ahead.

A moment passed. He hesitated, glancing back over his shoulder, as if expecting something or someone to stop him. His eyes flickered with an unspoken thought, something that hovered in his mind, catching his breath for a second.

With a sigh of relief, he finally lit the cigarette. The flame danced for a second before settling into a faint glow, the fire within him finally ready to be put out. He took a long, deliberate drag, letting the smoke fill his lungs like a temporary reprieve from the weight that had been pressing down on him.

"Ah, bliss." He murmured to himself.

His voice dropped to a whisper, barely audible in the silence of the brown and frosted glass laden hallway. A small smile crept across his face.

"My story will be told."

December, 2024

"*To discover the essence of true humanity, you must first question it. For what sets us apart is not our existence, but our perseverance. It is in our relentless will to endure, to rise despite the struggle, that we find what it truly means to be human.*"

- Dame Frida Galloway

ABOUT THE AUTHOR

Hussein Zohair is the mind behind this book—a raw collection of prose and poetry written over years as both a release and a reckoning, confronting his personal demons, one line at a time.

Writing, for Hussein, is both a passion and a peculiar lifeline. He's not entirely convinced of his own skill—often wondering if he's more of a writer by stubbornness than talent. Yet, he persists, pen in hand, wringing out thoughts unformed and stories unspoken. Through each poem and narrative, he channels the frustration he keeps tightly coiled within, much of it stemming from his lifelong struggle with a stammer.

This struggle is what first compelled him to pick up a pen, finding in writing the voice that often eludes him in speech. He explored more of this journey in his first novel, *Journeying James*, dialling up his own experiences into a tale that blends humour with heartache—mostly heartache.

Hussein sees his life much like a walnut—rough-edged and unpolished yet holding potential when given the right touch.

Thank you for reading this book, and if you have any questions about it, or my process, or have strong feedback that needs to be fed back, then do not hesitate to reach out to me on my personal email address: **husseinzohair@hotmail.com** or message me directly on my instagram handle: HusseinZooT. I'm super responsive. Really.

DISCLAIMER

All names, characters, and situations depicted in this book are the product of the author's imagination. Any resemblance to actual persons, living or deceased, or real-life situations is entirely coincidental. This work has not been inspired by any other medium or real-life events.

THANK YOU

9 789369 538799

Printed by Libri Plureos GmbH in Hamburg,
Germany